Smoking and Salt Curing

What You Need to Know About Preserving Meat, Game, Fish, and More!

Contents

INTRODUCTION 1
CHAPTER 1: INTRODUCTION TO FOOD PRESERVATION 3
    HISTORY OF FOOD PRESERVATION 4
    PRINCIPLES OF FOOD PRESERVATION 5
    DETECTING SPOILED FOOD 5
    CAUSES OF FOOD SPOILAGE 6
    IMPORTANCE OF FOOD PRESERVATION 7
        Reduces the Risk of Contamination 7
        Retains Quality 8
        Increases Shelf-Life 8
CHAPTER 2: METHODS OF FOOD PRESERVATION 9
    FREEZING 10
    CANNING 11
    DRYING 12
    FERMENTING 13
    SALTING 14
    PICKLING 15
    CURING 16
    SMOKING 17
    SEALING 18
    POTTING 19

    Tips To Remember... 19
CHAPTER 3: SMOKING MEAT.. 22
    Methods of Smoking 22
    Benefits of Smoking Meats... 23
    Risks to Consider.. 24
CHAPTER 4: BASIC THINGS TO NOTE BEFORE SMOKING 26
    Consider the Cut of the Meat 27
    Selecting the Wood... 27
    Select the Smoking Method 28
    Brining 29
    Select the Smoker 29
    Stick Burners 29
    Electric Smokers 30
    Pellet Smokers 30
    Gas Smokers.. 31
    Kettle Grills 31
    Charcoal Smokers 32
CHAPTER 5: SALT CURING.. 34
    Curing Agents and Mixtures 35
    Benefits of Curing 36
    Risks to Remember 36
CHAPTER 6: BASIC THINGS TO NOTE BEFORE SALT CURING....... 39
    Types of Salts to Use... 39
    Curing Options to Consider 42
        Dry Curing... 42
        Wet Curing 42
        Injecting... 43
    Equipment Needed.. 43
    Tips to Remember 43
CHAPTER 7: GUIDELINES FOR MEAT PRESERVATION 45
    Selecting The Meat 46
    Curing 46
    Dry Cure 47
    Wet Cure... 48

 Smoking 49

 Storage 49

CHAPTER 8: GUIDELINES FOR GAME PRESERVATION 51

 Aging 52

 Curing 53

 Smoking 53

 Storage 54

CHAPTER 9: PRESERVING YOUR FISH 55

 Selecting the Fish 55

 Preparing the Brine 56

 Preparing the Fish 56

 Place It in the Brine and Rinse 57

 Enjoy the Fish! 58

CHAPTER 10: PRESERVING YOUR POULTRY 59

 Select Good Quality Poultry 59

 Prepare the Brine Solution 60

 Inject the Brine 60

 Let the Poultry Soak 61

 Draining and Netting 61

 Smoking 62

 Complete the Cooking Process 62

 Storage 63

CHAPTER 11: POULTRY AND MEAT RECIPES 64

 Smoked Chicken 64

 Smoked Chicken Wings 67

 Smoked BBQ Korean Chicken Wings 69

 Smoked Herb Chicken 71

 Smoked Pulled Chicken 73

 Smoked Chicken Salad 75

 Brunswick Stew 76

 Smoked Turkey 78

 Smoked Chicken Breast 81

 Baked Potato and Smoked Chicken Casserole 83

 Penne with Smoked Chicken and Mascarpone 85

Chopped Salad with Smoked Brisket 87
Cured Beef and Pickle Sandwich 89
Loaded Grilled Italian Sandwich 90
Corned Beef Hash 92
Corned Beef Cottage Pie 93
Pepperoni Pasta Bake 95
Pepperoni Meatloaf 97
Smoked Pork Ribs 99
Smoked Pork Tenderloin 101
Smoked Pulled Pork 103
Smoked Brisket 105
Coffee-Rubbed Texas-Style Brisket 106
Irish Smoked Beef Brisket 108
Pulled Chuck Roast with Grilled Onions 110
Smoked Lamb Ribs 112
Smoked Meatloaf 113
Beef Salami 115
Herbed Sausage 116
Mexican Chorizo 118
Smoked Pastrami 120
Salt Cured Ham (Old-Fashioned Preserving) 123
Canadian Bacon 125
Deli Style Corned Beef 126
Pepperoni 127
German-Style Cured Pork Chops (Gepockelte) 129
Salt Beef 130
Cured Corned Beef 132
Potato Cakes Stuffed with Cured Meats 134
Stir-Fried Bamboo Shoots and Cured Ham 136

CHAPTER 12: FISH AND GAME RECIPES 137
Smoked and Cured Salmon with Orange Zest 137
Smoked Trout 139
Smoked Sturgeon 140
Smoked King Crab Legs 142

SMOKED TILAPIA 144
CURED SALMON GRAVLAX 145
KELP-CURED BLUE MACKEREL WITH FENNEL SALAD 147
MARINATED AND SMOKED VENISON TENDERLOIN 149
SMOKED VENISON JERKY 151
BRINED AND SMOKED WILD BOAR SHOULDER ROAST 153
SMOKED WHOLE QUAIL 155
SMOKED PHEASANT BREAST 157
SMOKED DUCK BREAST 158
MAPLE-SMOKED DUCK BREASTS 160
GOOSE PASTRAMI 161
SMOKED CORNISH GAME HENS 163
WILD GAME BACKSTRAP 164
SUGAR CURED FERAL HOG 166
SMOKED MACKEREL SALAD 168

CONCLUSION 169
HERE'S ANOTHER BOOK BY DION ROSSER THAT YOU MIGHT LIKE 170
REFERENCES 171

Introduction

The art of preserving meat, fish, game, and poultry is not a modern concept. Our early ancestors worldwide were known to preserve the fish and game they harvested to prolong its shelf life. In tropical regions, they used sun drying, and in colder regions, different meats were frozen using ice. Even though these techniques seem rudimentary, they paved the way for modern methods of preserving food. Food preservation includes a variety of techniques designed to avoid food spoilage due to different factors.

The most popular food preservation methods are smoking and salt curing. You can pretty much smoke and cure everything ranging from freshly caught game and fish to store-bought meats! The sky is truly the limit once you get the hang of it. "Smoking and Salt Curing: What You Need to Know About Preserving Meat, Game, Fish, and More!" will teach you how to do it all!

Whether you are a hunter, or an angler looking to cure and smoke your fresh catch, or a home cook interested in making delicious smoked meats at home, this is the perfect book for you. This book will act as your guide every step of the way. This book is your one-stop-shop for all information from helping you understand the history, meaning, elements, and methods of food preservation to learning in detail about smoking and salt curing. You will be introduced to the basics of smoking and salt curing before moving on to learning the guidelines for meat, game, fish, and poultry preservation.

Once you are armed with all the theoretical knowledge you need, you will explore the delicious recipes in this book. All the recipes are divided into different categories based on protein. These recipes are not only easy to understand but are simple to follow. You can start whipping up delicious meals at home in no time! You need only to gather the required ingredients after selecting a recipe that appeals to you. Follow the simple instructions, and voila!

So, are you excited to learn about the art of food preservation? If yes, let's get started immediately.

Chapter 1: Introduction to Food Preservation

Our ancestors were used to oscillating between periods of bounty and scarcity. The dire need to make it through scarcity acted as the catalyst that triggered preserving food. With the advent of agriculture and modern farming practices, the concept of famine is slowly vanishing from modern memory. However, there is still a need to keep food fresh from the time it is harvested until consumption. This is where food preservation techniques step into the picture. Whether it is to increase the shelf life, reduce the risk of contamination by pathogens, or retain the natural qualities of food items, food preservation serves various purposes.

Food preservation is a process that prevents decay or food spoilage, making it fit for storage and future use. It is also known as the state a food has managed to retain over a prolonged period without contamination traces. This, of course, while holding on to its natural properties in flavor, nutritional value, texture, and taste.

History of Food Preservation

From the moment food is harvested, it starts degrading. Our early ancestors, for the sake of survival, had to ensure they had sufficient sustenance to get through the cold months. They froze meat on ice in the freezing climate while the food was dried under the sun in tropical regions. This primary food preservation technique gave them the confidence and security required to put down their roots and form communities. They no longer had to worry about instantly consuming fresh kill or new harvest. Instead, they preserved it for later.

Due to the extremely cold temperatures in some regions, freezing was the ideal method for preservation. This eventually led to the invention of ice houses for storing the ice needed to preserve food. This later was transformed into iceboxes – further modified in the late 1800s for freezing foods. Clarence Birdseye, an American inventor and naturalist, discovered that frozen vegetables and fruits taste better when they were quickly frozen at relatively low temperatures.

As civilizations grew and developed, science also prospered. One of the novel techniques for preserving food was canning. A vacuum seal is created within the canning jar after the food is processed at high temperatures and cooled down. This technique destroys pathogens and inactivates any enzymes present within the ingredients. Foods that are canned and vacuum-sealed properly ensure microorganisms cannot enter the jar. This technique was introduced by a French man named Nicolas Appert during the 1790s.

During Napoleon's reign, in 1795, a significant reward was offered to anyone who could develop a new method to preserve food. Appert was given this reward in 1809 when he discovered canning for preserving foods. He believed the success of canning was because all air was eliminated during the preserving process, increasing the shelf life of food. Louis Pasteur proved him wrong in 1864 after discovering a direct relationship between pathogens and food spoilage.

Another notable achievement in the field of food preservation was the contribution made by Robert Ayers in 1812. He opened the first cannery in the United States. In 1858 the Mason jar was patented by John L. Mason. These achievements paved the way for several other innovations in the field of home food preservation. In 1915, Alexander H. Kerr patented a two-piece metal canning lid still used today. The popularity of home food preservation has not died down with time.

Principles of Food Preservation

With food preservation, some simple principles are standard regardless of the method used.

The first principle of food preservation is to prevent or possibly delay the decomposition of food by keeping microorganisms or pathogens away from it. It essentially means using different techniques to remove traces of microorganisms, prevent their growth, or destroy them.

The second principle is preventing self-decomposition of food or delaying it for as long as possible. Whether it is the destruction of enzymes or delaying any chemical reactions, this simple process prevents food from decomposing on its own.

The third principle of food preservation is to prevent any damage caused due to physical or external reasons such as mechanical causes or damage caused by rodents or insects.

Detecting Spoiled Food

Whether it was takeout or a home-cooked meal, chances are there would have been some leftovers. Maybe the food didn't taste as fresh as it did the previous night, or you stumbled across a mold-covered casserole during routine cleaning. Learning to identify whether the food has gone bad or not is a helpful skill. If you don't want an upset stomach or something more severe, never eat food that's gone bad. Besides this, identifying whether something specific has gone bad or not can reduce food wastage and help save a few dollars.

The most obvious sign the food has gone bad is mold. Meats and dairy products are especially susceptible to mold. From a layer of white fuzz to black or green spots, mold comes in different forms. As soon as you see mold, throw the food item away. Similarly, discard all foods coated with a slimy film. If the meat looks and feels damp, it is a bad idea to put it in your mouth! Watch out for any changes in the texture and color of food. If the item has been discolored, it is a clear sign of oxidation. One final tip to identify whether the food has gone bad or not is the smell. If the food smells rancid or different from how it smelled previously, it has gone bad!

Causes of Food Spoilage

The primary motivation for preserving food is to increase its shelf life and prevent instant degradation. From the moment the producers harvest or slaughter flood, it started degrading. The most common reasons for food spoilage are physical damages and chemical changes.

If the food is damaged, bruised, or even punctured due to external factors, it is termed *physical damage*. Any damage caused by microorganisms or insects is included in this. At times, the physical damage caused by insects – such as puncturing or bruising the foods – can increase the risk of pathogen contamination.

But oxidation, growth of microbes, and change in enzymes within food products are known as chemical changes. If iron is left exposed to elements such as water and air, rust forms through a process known as oxidation. This process applies to food too. Oxidized food generally turns rancid.

Enzymes are helpful chemicals present in animals and plants responsible for their growth and functioning. Even after harvest, these enzymes don't stop working. This reaction of enzymes changes the texture and flavor of the ingredients.

The third common cause of food spoilage is microbial growth. The three common microorganisms that harm food are mold, bacteria, and yeast. The greenish spots on old bread or a fuzzy white layer on dairy products signify mold growth. Mold doesn't discriminate and can easily spoil all types of foods. If the food seems slimy or starts bubbling, it is a sign of yeast growth. As with mold, yeast doesn't discriminate either. Another pathogen that spoils food is bacteria. Bacteria tend to multiply rapidly and make the food unsafe for consumption.

Importance of Food Preservation

What pops into your head when you think of food preservation? Do you perhaps think of canned or dehydrated foods, or maybe frozen foods? Well, there is so much more to it than this. Food preservation is not a new concept, and it has been around since time immemorial.

Whenever you are learning something new, the best way to motivate yourself is by concentrating on its benefits. Here are all the benefits of preserving food.

Reduces the Risk of Contamination

Perhaps the most obvious benefit of food preservation is it reduces the risk of contamination by pathogens. Whether it is salmonella, E Coli, or other pathogens, different types of bacteria tend to spoil and degrade food. By preserving it, you are essentially inhibiting the growth of such harmful pathogens. It, in turn, reduces the risk of food-borne diseases.

Retains Quality

An important benefit of food preservation is that it helps retain the quality of the ingredients. When food starts deteriorating, as it normally does with time, it goes bad. If you notice any signs discussed in the previous section, it is unfit for consumption. The food is unsafe to eat, and its taste, appearance, and texture are significantly altered. Food preservation techniques help retain the natural qualities of ingredients, including their nutritional value, texture, and taste, to a great degree.

Increases Shelf-Life

Another benefit of food preservation is that you get to enjoy seasonal ingredients all year round. It also helps reduce your grocery bills as wasting food is quite expensive. Using different preservation methods, you can save meats, vegetables, fish, and pretty much anything you desire well past their expected expiration dates.

Besides all this, preserving food can increase your sense of satisfaction. When you learn about the different techniques in this book and follow the simple recipes, you can start preserving food in no time! You will certainly feel a sense of pride when you do the job and do it well!

Chapter 2: Methods of Food Preservation

The concept of refrigeration became commonplace only during the last couple of decades. Before that, different techniques were employed for increasing the shelf life of foods. Some of these techniques date back thousands of years. Drying, salting, and pickling are food preservation techniques that not only increase the shelf life of foods but change their flavor, appearance, and texture. The change isn't undesirable, however, like the one caused when food goes bad. They are classic techniques and are still favored today because of their unique transformative properties. In this chapter, we'll look at some of the most common food preservation techniques.

Freezing

When foods are chilled and stored at least 10°F, it is known as freezing. All foods, including dairy products, vegetables, eggs, nuts, seafood, and fully cooked foods, can be stored using this method. To try your hand at freezing, understand that it differs from tossing the ingredients into the freezer compartment of a regular refrigerator. A regular refrigerator supports temperatures between 10-32°F while freezing requires a temperature of at least 10°F. It is an easy process, provided you can invest in a deep freezer, which is a rather expensive purchase.

Canning

Canning essentially includes two processes known as pasteurizing and vacuum sealing. The first is pasteurizing, where food is heated for a specific duration at a specific temperature to eliminate pathogens, including harmful bacteria. This cooking process also prevents the activity of enzymes in the food. Once the ingredients are pasteurized, they can come to room temperature before moving on to the final stage - vacuum sealing. The pasteurized foods are placed in special glass jars designed for this purpose. Most foods, including seafood, meats, vegetables, fruit, and even some cooked foods, can be stored using this technique.

Drying

Perhaps one of the most used preservation techniques for prolonging the shelf life of foods is drying. With drying, foods are dehydrated to remove excess moisture present within. This process reduces the risk of any microbial activity. Fruits, vegetables, legumes, nuts, and even seafood are commonly preserved using this technique.

Fermenting

Fermenting is a very common process that encourages cultivating good pathogens that preserve the food instead of spoiling them. Different types of foods, including vegetables, meat, seafood fruits, common legumes, eggs, and dairy products, can be easily fermented. Yes, you are increasing the growth of desirable bacteria and other pathogens to discourage the growth of unhealthy ones. For instance, wine is made from fermented grapes, yogurt is only fermented milk, while cured sausages refer to fermented meats.

Salting

Salting was quite a popular method of preserving food before the advent of modern refrigeration. It helps preserve food by drawing out all the moisture present within. When there is no moisture left, bacteria and other pathogens cannot develop or survive. It, in turn, increases the shelf life of the ingredients. There are two types of salting - dry and wet salting. In dry salting, food is covered in salt and left in a cool and dry place. When the salt draws out moisture present in the food, you might need to pour out the accumulated liquid and replace the lost salt.

But in wet curing, food is placed in a salt and water mixture known as brine. The ingredients are left to soak in the brine in a cool and dry place. More flavors can be easily incorporated into the foods by adding peppercorns or Juniper berries to the brine. Since the food is preserved in salt in one form or other, the result can be incredibly salty. So, the salted food might need to be reintroduced to water or reconstituted to remove the excess salt to be fit for consumption.

Pickling

Pickling helps preserve food by using an edible antimicrobial solution that prevents the growth of pathogens. Food is immersed in a solution that contains alcohol, salt, or acid. The most common foods that are pickled include eggs, legumes, fruits, vegetables, certain meats, and seafood. You need no special equipment for pickling. However, if pickled foods are stored carelessly or preserved at room temperature, they can become unsafe for consumption. This technique usually combines other preservation methods such as refrigeration, canning, or fermentation.

Curing

Curing involves flavoring and preserving food, especially fish and meat, by adding a mixture of salt, sugar, and nitrites or nitrates. Salt is believed to inhibit the growth of microorganisms responsible for decomposing food. It helps draw the water out of microbial cells through a process known as osmosis. If the population of bacteria is reduced, food automatically becomes safer for consumption. Curing encourages the growth of desirable bacteria belonging to the Lactobacillus genus. Here's a fun fact- bacteria belonging to this genus are commonly found within our digestive tract and are good for our digestive health.

This brings us to the next ingredient commonly used in curing-sugar. Sugar also limits the growth of bacteria and their existing population. Even if certain types of bacteria are considered good, too much of anything is seldom good. Sugar adds an interesting flavor and smell to the preserved food, making it more enjoyable. The nitrates or nitrites kill harmful pathogens while adding a tangy flavor to the meat. They also help retain a pinkish or reddish tinge to the meat. The most used nitrate is sodium or potassium nitrate. These nitrates bind with iron atoms present within the food and prevent oxidation. You will learn more about this technique in the subsequent chapters.

Smoking

Smoking is a wonderful preservation technique that improves the appearance, texture, and flavor of the food stored. It is also used as a drying technique. Smoking pairs perfectly with curing and acts as a flavor enhancer. Compared to unsmoked meats, the likelihood of smoked meats turning rancid, getting oxidized, or growing mold is quite low. You will learn more about this food preservation technique in the later chapters.

Sealing

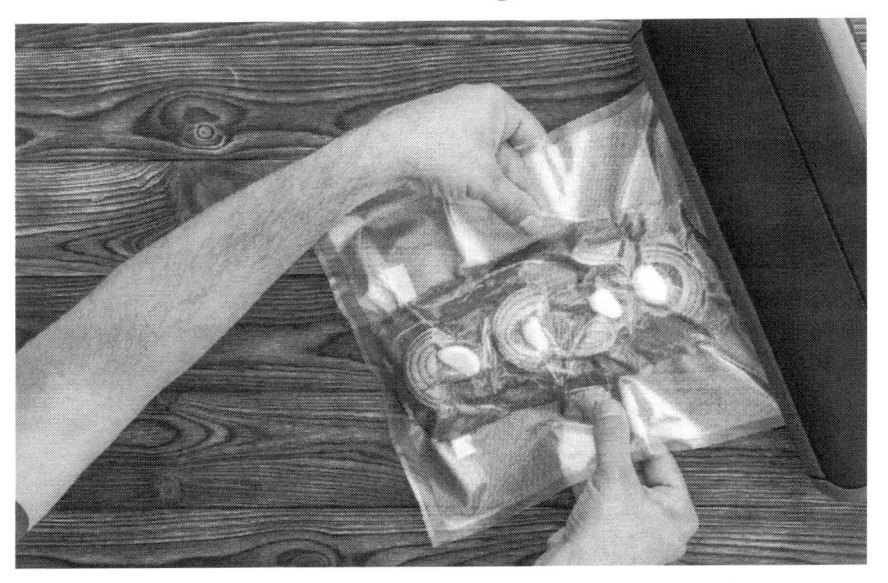

Sealing is a food preservation process where the air is kept out to delay the decaying processes triggered by different pathogens. This technique simply delays but does not stop the process of decay, though. Sealing is commonly used with other preservation techniques such as freezing and drying. Fat and vacuum sealing are the most common sealing techniques.

Potting

Potting is an old British food preservation technique still used in certain parts of France. The idea is simple. The meat is first prepared and thoroughly cooked before shifting for storage. After the meat is fully prepped, it is placed in a ceramic crock or any other pot for storage. The crock used is fully sterilized to deter the growth of bacteria. After the meat is placed in it, all fats collected are melted and poured into the crock. As soon as the fat covering the meat solidifies, it is ready for storage. The crock is then stored in a cool and dry location, such as a root cellar.

Tips To Remember

Here are some food safety guidelines you should always follow while curing and smoking meats. It doesn't matter whether you are interested in preserving poultry or fish. These rules are still applicable. Please follow them for your own safety.

The first rule is to thoroughly wash your hands with soap and water for at least 20 seconds before and after working. Always wash your hands after changing tasks. If you do any specific activity which can contaminate your hands, don't forget to wash them. The same rules apply even if you sneeze or use the washroom.

Ensure the equipment and workspace you will use to prepare the food are completely clean before you start using them. Sterilize all the equipment with hot soapy water to ensure there are no traces of pathogens. Remember, the idea is to preserve the meat. If these meats are exposed to pathogens in any form, the risk of contamination obviously increases.

Whenever you are using cutting boards, always wash them first. Wash them with hot water, soap, and rinse them. You can also sanitize them using a solution made of water and chlorine. Add one tablespoon of chlorine bleach to one gallon of water or one teaspoon for 4 cups of water. Spray or dip the cutting boards in the solution and let them air dry.

If you are using any frozen meat, ensure it is perfectly thawed before you use it. To thaw the meat, you should not leave it outside and let it thaw. Instead, place it in the refrigerator at a temperature of around 40°F. If you use any raw meat, always keep separate cutting boards for it. It's not just the cutting board. The work surfaces need to be different too. You can always color coordinate the boards to remember which ones are used for different types of meat. Raw meat can quickly become a breeding spot for all sorts of pathogens, and unless you are careful, you cannot reduce the risk of contamination, especially cross-contamination.

Before you preserve meat, ensure it is perfectly cooked. To do this, you must check its internal temperature. You will learn about the different internal cooking temperatures for different types of meat in the following chapters. Pay extra attention to the temperatures for cooking and storing them. You can use a food thermometer to check whether the meat is cooked properly or not.

In fact, investing in a food thermometer is a good idea if you want to smoke meat.

After cooking, ensure you let the meat cool down to at least room temperature before preserving. Never put warm or hot meat in the fridge. While storing it in the freezer, always use freezer-safe containers and food-grade plastic. The stored meat should not be directly exposed to air.

Chapter 3: Smoking Meat

As explained, there are several preservation techniques commonly used for increasing the shelf life of different products. One such food preservation technique is smoking. This is a great way to treat foods by preventing any spoilage caused by pathogens. Smoking is a preservation technique that promotes the shelf life of the product and improves its flavor profile. It helps flavor, cook, and preserves the food by exposing it to steady smoke. Smoke is generated by burning plant material such as wood or even hardwood. While it is mostly a commercial process, it can be carried out at home provided you have the right equipment.

Methods of Smoking

The two methods are commonly used for smoking are hot and cold smoking.

In hot smoking, the food is directly exposed to smoke in a controlled environment. Smoked foods can be cooked or reheated as and when required. They are also ready for consumption with no further cooking. The usual temperature range for hot smoking is between 125-180°F. When food is exposed to this temperature, it's normally cooked internally. The ideal temperature for most cooked meats is around 180°F. So, if the ingredients are exposed to hot smoke, you can consume them immediately. Foods tend to retain their moisture and texture at this heat level while a smoky flavor is added. If the temperature increases beyond this, foods can lose their moisture, and the fat starts drying. Usually, smoking is used combined with other preservation techniques such as curing or drying. For example, once foods are salt-cured, they are smoked to increase their shelf life.

This brings us to the next smoking method known as cold smoking. This is more of a flavor enhancer than a cooking technique. It is commonly used for improving the flavor of chicken breast, pork chops, scallops, steak, and even salmon. The temperature used for this is between 68-90°F. The temperature is maintained at this level with the aim of moisture retention. It is not meant for food preservation. It's simply about adding a smoky flavor to the food. So, foods that are cold smoked shouldn't be consumed immediately, and instead, they need to be cured before they are cold smoked. When meats are cured, the moisture in them is removed, which prevents bacterial growth. Once the meat is cured and preserved using any other technique, it can be cold smoked.

Benefits of Smoking Meats

Smoke is believed to have antioxidant and antimicrobial properties. This means that any pathogens present on the surface of meat are eliminated, as are their chances of reappearing. However, smoking cannot be used as a standalone preservation technique. The problem is that the compound of smoke only sticks to the outer surface of the food, and it does not penetrate the meat or the food you are trying to preserve. So, the antioxidant and antimicrobial properties of smoke are restricted to the external surfaces of the meat. This is why smoking needs to be combined with other preservation techniques such as salt curing or drying.

Whenever wood is burned, its smoke contains phenol and certain phenolic compounds believed to be natural antioxidants. Oxidation is a process that occurs when the structure of the molecules is changed due to oxygen exposure. A common example of damage caused by the oxidation of food is rancidity. Food goes bad when left exposed to the elements for prolonged periods. So, the helpful compounds in wood smoke curtail the rancidification of fats present in meat, fish, and even poultry. This, coupled with antimicrobial agents such as formaldehyde, acetic acid, and several other helpful organic acids, reduces the pH of smoke. The usual pH of smoke is around 2.5. This low level of pH makes it difficult for pathogens to survive.

Besides prolonging the shelf life of food, smoking also elevates the flavor profile. Smoked meats are simply delicious! Once the meats are smoked and preserved, they can be stored for up to one year at the right temperature! This gives you easy access to the required ingredients whenever you want to cook. This certainly makes the meat more appetizing and flavorful. The color of the meat also changes once it is smoked. The meats seem shinier and redder. This simply makes them more appealing.

Risks to Consider

Too much of anything is bad. Everything needs to be balanced in every aspect of your life, which is true for diet. Eating too much of anything is not good for your body. So, eating too much smoked food is certainly not good for you. A common reason is the active compounds released from wood during smoking dries out the food. This essentially means the substances from smoke are incorporated into your food. Increased consumption of smoked food is associated with an increased risk of different types of cancers. Read on to learn more about the disadvantages associated with smoking food.

Smoking is a tedious process that requires specific equipment and plenty of attention. It can be a little expensive in terms of the resources involved. Keeping the moisture content low must be a priority while smoking. If not, it increases the risk of pathogen contamination. While smoking, if the fire is too hot, or if there isn't sufficient heat or smoke, the meat can quickly go bad before it is properly smoked.

Potential carcinogens can also be present in smoked food. This is due to the transference process responsible for smoking. Apart from the helpful phenols released by burning wood, certain hydrocarbons known as polycyclic aromatic hydrocarbons (PAHs) are also released. PAHs are believed to be food contaminants that increase the risk of gastrointestinal cancer. In recent research undertaken by the American Chemical Society, a simple way to reduce the risk of exposure to carcinogens is by taking a leaf from the auto industry's playbook. The zeolite filters used in automobiles filter harmful compounds and reduce air pollution. By using such filters fitted to smokers, the risk of carcinogens can be reduced. Once again, it is important to note the real problem starts if you consume too much smoked meat. Eating it occasionally is not harmful.

However, it is worth noting that the research is not definitive, and more evidence is needed to prove the case.

Chapter 4: Basic Things to Note Before Smoking

The modern concept of smoking food is a continuation of an age-old technique of food preservation. Before chemical preservatives and refrigeration were invented, smoke was used to extend the shelf life of ingredients, especially meats. In the previous chapter, you were introduced to the different reasons smoke is believed to be a preservative. From acetic acid and formaldehyde to the low PH level, smoke has several antioxidant and antimicrobial properties that prolong its shelf life. It's not just about prolonging the shelf life, but it also reduces any risk of contamination.

These days, smoking is mostly about tenderizing meats and enhancing their flavor. However, it doesn't mean you can't use it to preserve food. Once you get the hang of smoking, don't restrict yourself to meat. These days, nuts, vegetables, fruits, and even different types of cheese are smoked! Before you smoke food, here are some important things you should consider.

Consider the Cut of the Meat

Whenever you think about smoking something, it's important to determine the ingredient you wish to smoke. From poultry and different types of meat to fish, different things can be smoked. Why is it important to consider the cut of the meat here? Depending on the thickness of the cut, the time required for smoking will differ. The most common cuts used for smoking include all the motion muscles. For instance, spareribs from the belly, loin, beef brisket, and ribs are the most common meat cuts chosen for smoking.

For smoking, it is always better to choose fatty cuts. Fat helps the meat absorb the delicious smoky flavors. So, whenever you choose any meat to smoke, look for cuts with plenty of fat and connective tissue. Choosing fattier cuts keeps the meat tender and moist. When the fat starts melting, it bastes the meat in its juices. This further elevates the flavor profile while easily incorporating the smokiness into the chosen meat.

As you read through the different chapters on food preservation discussed in this book, a point to remember is that smoking is the final step in the preservation process. Whether it is fish, poultry, meat, or game, the ingredients are first salt-cured before they are smoked.

Selecting the Wood

If you want good results from smoking, pay extra attention to the wood used. Yes, wood type plays an important role here. Different types of wood tend to pair with different flavors of the meat and would need to complement the flavor of the meat. Let us look at some common woods used for smoking.

Apple wood has a fruity and sweet taste. It is rather mild and pairs brilliantly well with poultry, ham, and fish. Another commonly used wood for smoking is alder. Alder has a delicate flavor profile and natural sweetness that elevates the flavor of pork, fish, poultry, and all other types of light meats. The best way to incorporate some hearty smokiness into red meats and ribs is to use hickory. This is the most popular word used in barbecues. Hickory's pungent and strong smell perfectly complements the hardness of red meats. This brings us to another commonly used wood- oak. Oak is ideal for large cuts of meat smoked for extended periods. It offers a good smoky flavor that is not overpowering. Whether it is brief brisket or game meats, this is a great choice of wood. Mesquite is also popular, but it can be overwhelming. Mesquite should be used just like peppers in cooking. It is ideal for short durations when used in combination with other woods.

Maple has a light and sweet taste that pairs well with ham and poultry. Be careful while using maple, however, because it can darken the color of meat. As with mesquite, maple is used with other woods such as oak and apple. Pecan has a pungent fruity flavor but use it sparingly. It also doesn't burn quite as hot as other woods, making it ideal for smoking larger cuts of meat. To improve the color of any meat, add some cherry wood. It pairs brilliantly with pork and beef.

If in doubt, always choose oak or alder. These are the safest bets for smoking meats.

Select the Smoking Method

As explained, there are two types of smoking methods available. Depending on the results you are trying to achieve, the smoking process you need to choose will differ. For instance, if you aim only to infuse the smell of smoke into the meat, choose cold smoking. On the other hand, if you want to cook the meat thoroughly, choose hot smoking.

Brining

During the smoking process, meat tends to dry out. This is one reason why placing the meat in brine is a wonderful idea. A solution of water and salt is known as brine. Depending on the cut of the meat, the quantity of brine required will differ. Brining meat is a great way of ensuring lean cuts of meat do not dry out during the smoking process. If you decide to brine the meat, it becomes easier to preserve it. If you are interested in immediately consuming the meat, this step is optional. You will learn more about using brine for different meats in the subsequent chapters.

Select the Smoker

Now that you have decided on your meat, how you want to smoke it, the type of wood, and when you want to consume it, all that's left for you to do is select the right smoker. Selecting the wood was one aspect of deciding how to go about the smoking process. So now, it's time to determine the smoker that will work well for you. The most common smokers on the market are gas-fired barbecue pits and electric ones.

Stick Burners

Stick burners rely solely on wood as their fuel source. In the previous section, you were introduced to the different types of wood paired with different meats. Carefully go through the list and select one combination that appeals to you. Once you have the wood ready, you simply need to place them on the stick burner. These burners require the most attention compared to all the others mentioned in this section. Because you need to pay constant attention to the food while it's on the burner, a steep learning curve is involved.

And most cheap variants from any local hardware or departmental store are not good at retaining heat and are rather flimsy. There are higher-end stick burners available made of heavy-duty materials. However, they can be rather expensive.

Electric Smokers

Electric smokers use an electric heating rod. It helps ignite the wood pellets present inside the smoker. The wood pellets serve a dual purpose here. They act as a heat source to cook the meat and as a flavor enhancer. When the wood pellets are placed into the firebox, the heat can be regulated using a thermostat. The heating element of these smokers produces smoke instead of an open flame. Since there is no combustion here, its smoke is different in flavor compared to live fire.

Pellet Smokers

These are similar to a pellet grill or a kitchen oven. They come with an embedded thermostat that can be used for regulating the smoker's temperature. All you need to do is simply place the smoker where you want, plug it into a socket, set the ideal temperature, and let the smoker do the rest. You don't have to constantly check on the smoker to ensure the meat doesn't burn, thanks to the adjustable thermostat. In a pellet smoker, pellets made of compressed sawdust are pushed into a firepot next to the smoker's internal mechanism, which then combusts in the firepot to produce the required heat and smoke. These smokers are incredibly easy to use. That said, the flavor produced by a live fire cannot be replaced or even duplicated by any other smoker models.

Gas Smokers

The next category of smokers includes gas-fired ones. As with electric smokers, these use propane or any other natural gas for ignition. The gas-fired units can be used for hot and cold smoking meats. These smokers usually have a water pan that helps retain moisture in the meat while cooking or smoking it. This means the meat isn't at risk of drying out quickly. Gas smokers offer great control over the cooking temperature, but they produce no smoke.

Kettle Grills

This is a live-fire piece of kitchen equipment that most home cooks are familiar with. If you are a little careful and use it smartly, it can be used for smoking meats at home. However, these grills are not ideal for slow-smoking meats. For instance, you can create an indirect heat source by restricting the charcoal or wood chips to one-half of the grill. You can place the meat on the other side. Similarly, keep a thermometer nearby to ensure the meat is cooking properly. You will learn more about the different cooking temperatures for different meats in the following chapters.

Charcoal Smokers

Charcoal smokers include the most popular smokers, such as the stainless-steel Weber Smokey Monkey, Pit Barrel cooker, other drum smokers, and ceramic kamado ovens such as the Big Green Egg. When compared to a stick burner, these don't require that much attention but are not entirely hands-off either. After the coal is lit, you will need to adjust the temperature using the built-in dampers for controlling the airflow. Most of the smoke will be produced from the charcoal, but you can always add some extra wood chips for flavoring the meat. While doing this, it's important to remember that wood smolders instead of combusting, and the smoke given out by it might not be as flavorful as those produced by a stick burner.

Charcoal is the fuel source for these smokers. Simply ignite the charcoal and leave it in the smoker until the ash is left. This is similar to grilling meats on a barbecue. The food must be placed on racks once the coal is hot enough. Close the smoker and let it cook. This is perfect for hot smoking meats.

If you are considering buying a smoker, there are a few factors you need to remember. The most obvious one is your budget. If you are just getting started with smoking meats, stick to the basics for now. Once you get the hang of it, you can always invest in a higher-end version. To learn to barbecue and smoke, starting with a charcoal smoker is a good idea. They are affordable and easy to use. The next factor to consider is the fuel type used by the smoker. This factor is in tandem with the previous one. Once again, it is better to stick with charcoal to get the hang of barbecuing and grilling meats.

But if convenience is the sole priority, a pellet smoker is a worthy investment. Consider the usual size of the meat to be smoked before buying a smoker. If you are interested in smoking large cuts of meat or game meat, you will need a considerably bigger smoker.

Chapter 5: Salt Curing

How do you usually keep your meat safe? The answer is you refrigerate it. Well, refrigeration is a relatively new invention. Before refrigerators were introduced, curing was the technique most used to preserve meat. Salt-cured meats are popular even today, not just out of necessity but also because of their unique taste. You can make different types of cured meats such as bacon, sausage, ham, and corned beef at home if you know how curing works.

Curing is essentially a technique that uses salt to preserve the meat. Remember, in the previous chapter, we mentioned that pathogen contamination or growth of living organisms such as bacteria results in food spoilage? Salt helps kill them and prevents this process. If any pathogens start ingesting the meat and metabolizing it, the meat's texture, color, and flavor start changing. These are all telltale signs of food spoilage.

So, how exactly does salt help preserve the food? Salt removes all the moisture or water present within the meat cells through a process known as osmosis. Osmosis has two beneficial effects. The first effect is it dries the meat, and the second is it kills all the pathogens. It's important to remember that salt here doesn't mean regular table salt. Instead, it refers to a combination of salt, salt cures, and a little sugar.

The most common types of salt-cured meats are bacon, ham, and corned beef. Apart from this, pancetta, liverwurst, summer sausage, salami, and chorizo are also salt-cured meats. Even if the time taken to salt-cured meats is stretched to several weeks, the flavor it produces is worth it. During curing, different enzymes in the meat undergo various chemical changes that build the meat's flavor. Besides this, the salt used in curing further elevates its natural flavor. This, coupled with sugar, herbs, and spices, further balance the flavors and elevates them to the next level. If salted meat is smoked later, it creates a wonderful and well-rounded flavor profile. Salted meats aren't cooked. Some salted meats are further dried to ensure they are fit for consumption.

Curing Agents and Mixtures

The most common curing agents are salt, nitrates, nitrites, and sugar. You also have the option of purchasing readymade cure mixtures. Salt was commonly used for curing meats before saltpeter replaced it. It's believed that during the 1600s, it was discovered that a mixture of saltpeter and salt was a better and effective way to preserve meat. The potassium nitrate present in the saltpeter kills bacteria responsible for botulism. The nitrate also retains the pink color of the meat. This is what our ancestors believed. It turns out, the reasons for the pink color and the extended shelf life are not as straightforward.

You will learn more about the different types of salts used, commercially produced curing mixture, and alternatives in the next chapter.

Benefits of Curing

The most obvious benefit of salt curing is to prolong the shelf life of ingredients. For instance, if the meats are properly cured and later dried or smoked, their shelf life increases by a couple of months. If stored at the right temperature, cured meats are fit for consumption for almost a year! This is a great way to preserve meats, poultry, fish, and even game meats.

Another advantage of salt curing is it kills any harmful pathogens in the meat. The salt dries out the meat and removes any traces of moisture. When this happens, the pathogens are automatically killed. The meat becomes inhospitable for disease-causing pathogens.

Salting is also a great way to elevate the flavor and texture of certain meats. Once the meats are cured, they can be cooked in different ways. For instance, bacon tastes different from a regular strip of pork belly, doesn't it? This is due to the curing process it undergoes.

Risks to Remember

It was a popular belief that nitrites and nitrates have carcinogenic properties. This widespread belief resulted from a rather flawed experiment conducted back in the 70s. Even though this risk has been debunked as a myth, the damage was done. In 2003, WHO (World Health Organization) issued a clarification stating there was no association between cancer risk and nitrites or nitrates. Most natural foods, including vegetables such as carrots, spinach, lettuce, and celery, are sources of nitrites. So, don't worry about nitrites.

Perhaps the most significant risk you must take into consideration while salt curing meats is the presence of pathogens. Clostridium botulinum is the bacteria responsible for Botulism. Botulism can be deadly, and it is more dangerous than food pathogens such as E Coli or salmonella. Botulism is a food-borne illness, and the bacteria causing it is commonly found in soil. The microbe by itself is not harmful. The problem is with the neurotoxin it produces. Bacteria can produce this toxin in an anaerobic environment.

Any environment devoid of oxygen is known as an anaerobic environment. For instance, the environment inside the tissue of cured meat or meat being cured is anaerobic. With fresh meat, you don't have to worry about botulism. The real trouble starts when you are curing and preserving meat. To prevent botulism, there are three methods available. The first is salting and dehydrating. The second method is to reduce the environments' pH or create an acidic condition that inhibits the microbe's growth. The third idea is to pressure-can the meat. Whenever you are using any meat, you can avoid the risk of Botulism by curing and then smoking it.

One way to kill this bacterium is by submerging it in brine or keeping it in the dry salt curing mix. This, coupled with temperature control, will make the cured meats safe for consumption. Curing should take place in a temperature-controlled environment. The ideal temperature to be maintained is between 36-40°F to prevent the growth of pathogens.

Cured meats are safe for consumption. That said, those with any existing cardiovascular disorders, including high levels of cholesterol and blood pressure, should severely restrict their consumption of cured meat. Cured meat is rich in sodium, and this can further worsen any existing blood pressure problems.

Always keep the salt cures out of the reach of children. Nitrites and nitrates aren't carcinogenic agents, but children shouldn't directly consume them. Their digestive systems, especially the helpful bacteria in the digestive tract, aren't yet developed to digest nitrites and nitrates.

Don't try to cure meat at home without using curing salt. Without the salt cure, the desirable action of nitrites and nitrates doesn't occur. Unless the nitrites in the cure react with the meat, the meat proteins aren't broken down, and if this doesn't happen, nitric oxide isn't produced. Nitric oxide prevents the growth of harmful pathogens and removes all their traces. You will learn more about all this in the next chapter.

Chapter 6: Basic Things to Note Before Salt Curing

You might be quite tempted to skip to the recipes about preserving different ingredients. Before you do this, it is important to know the basic steps involved in salt curing. It is not just about understanding the concepts. You must also understand the different methods, types of curing salts, and so on. If you are a beginner, do not skip this chapter.

Types of Salts to Use

To understand how curing works and the different salt you can use, you need a brief chemistry lesson. When selecting the salt used for curing, there are many options available, and the evidence is often conflicting. In the past, regular salt was used to cure meat, but during the 1600s, saltpeter was added to the curing mixture. Saltpeter is the common name for sodium nitrate or potassium nitrate. However, saltpeter does not directly preserve the food. Salt is mainly used to preserve the food. However, certain types of bacteria can't be killed by salt alone. As such, saltpeter is added to protect against them. Bacteria in the food eat the nitrates in the saltpeter, and in this process, nitrites are produced. After this, another reaction further occurs, which turns these nitrites into nitric oxide. Nitric oxide starts bonding with various proteins present in the meat. This makes the meat pink and reduces the risk of oxidation. Nitric oxide is essentially preserving the meat while killing the deadly spores of Botulism and other harmful bacteria. Whenever you are using saltpeter, it is always used along with salt. Saltpeter is not a salt substitute.

This brings us to something that is commonly known as pink salt or Prague powder. It is another name for saltpeter, used for curing meat. It is known as pink salt because a food coloring is added to it, so consumers do not mistake it for normal salt. The pink hue of the cured meat resulting from salt-curing isn't associated with the red dye mixed in the cure. Remember, it is the activation of nitric oxide, which gives the meat a pink hue. Prague powder #1 and Prague powder #2 are two types of pink salts. They are also known as pink salt #1 and pink salt #2, respectively. The former contains around 93% common table salt, and the rest is sodium nitrite. If you are cooking meat, poultry, or fish after curing it, choose Prague powder #1. But pink salt #2 contains 4% sodium nitrate, 6.25% sodium nitrite, and the rest is table salt. This is used as a dry cure for meats that will not undergo any further cooking processes, such as prosciutto.

Besides this, some recipes use Morton Tender Quick. It is a mixture of salt, sodium nitrite, sugar, and sodium nitrate. It is not dyed pink like its counterparts. If you are using this at home, ensure that you keep it separate from the regular table salt. A common mistake most beginners make is that they believe all curing salts are the same. Curing salts are not interchangeable, so please do not make this mistake. If a curing recipe uses a specific curing salt, follow the instructions. Don't try to change it. The salts are chosen based on the preservation process involved.

Now that you understand the different types of curing salts used for food preservation, it's time to address some worries most have about curing salts. It's a common misconception that curing salts are extremely toxic. Curing salts are only toxic in large and excessive quantities. Curing salts are not meant for direct consumption. You're not supposed to inhale it or rub it over your eyes. It should be kept out of children's reach. Don't worry about all of this because home curing recipes do not call for such massive quantities of salt. Also, you are not exposed to it constantly, and therefore, it does not threaten your health.

Another common worry regarding nitrites is their association with an increased risk of cancer. Nitrites are found in natural foods. They are more common than you might have believed. For instance, you will consume more nitrites in a single serving of spinach than from a serving of salami.

The only concern to worry about when curing meats is the risk of botulism. Apart from that, there's nothing else to worry about. The risk of Botulism reduces when you follow the curing recipe properly and maintain the required salting and smoking temperatures.

There are alternatives to curing salts. The only reason to use curing salts is to eliminate all traces of Botulism spores in the meat. You can cure using regular salt, but there are a few issues you need to be aware of. The presence of iodine in regular or table salt is a major issue. Table salt is always iodized, and iodine can lend a weird taste to the cured meat. Other anti-clumping active ingredients in table salt make the dry cure lumpy. If you use it to make the brine, there might be sediments in it. When using regular salt for curing the meat, stick to the recipe and ensure you choose non-iodized salt.

If you are using regular salt, pay attention to the size of the salt granules. This can affect the amount of salt that goes into a recipe. For instance, a cup of kosher salt is about 5-8 ounces, while one cup of table salt equals 10-ounces. So, one cup of table salt is a different measurement as kosher salt. An efficient way to measure the ingredients whenever you are curing meats at home is to use a weighing scale.

If you are looking for a natural source of nitrate, choose celery juice. Celery juice has natural nitrates. In the curing process, celery juice triggers a reaction similar to saltpeter. However, this isn't a substitute for the results produced using saltpeter.

Curing Options to Consider

You have three options for curing meats using salt. Namely, dry curing, wet curing, and injecting. The safest option available for curing at home is wet curing. Let us learn more about these options and how they work.

Dry Curing

The most common preservation technique for curing meats is dry curing. Remember when you were introduced to the different curing mixtures in the previous section? Now, you simply need to rub the meat with the curing mixture, place it in a container, and cover it with more curing mix. The meat must then be placed in the refrigerator or any other cold space where a steady temperature of 36-40°F can be maintained. Regulating the temperature and humidity are the most crucial aspects of curing meat. So, pay extra attention to it.

Wet Curing

To cure limited quantities of meat, wet curing should be your go-to option. It is especially helpful if you will be cooking the cured meat again. For this, you need to make a brine solution and simply submerge the meat in it. The brine removes the excess moisture and helps create an ideal balanced that prevents pathogen breeding. You can easily regulate the salt used with this method. This method ensures that the salt has evenly seeped into the meat and there are no salt pockets created in it. While wet curing the meat, store it in the fridge or freezer. The meat must always stay submerged in the brine, and you must keep turning it every few days, so it is evenly exposed to the brine. The meat shouldn't be exposed to air. Preferably, use a separate storage area for curing meats to prevent cross-contamination.

Injecting

As the name suggests, you will essentially be injecting salty brine into the meat using a syringe. It is slightly difficult to ensure the brine is evenly distributed with this method, especially if you don't have the required professional equipment. As a DIY solution, this rarely is recommended. One common problem with this method is it can create salt pockets in the meat.

Equipment Needed

Whether it is dry curing or smoking meats, you'll need some basic equipment. The most important aspect of curing meats is a cool area or a fridge. Temperature regulation is a crucial part of curing. If you're not careful, improper temperature increases the risk of pathogens breeding on your meats. This makes the final product unfit for consumption. The usual temperature required for curing and storing meats is less than 40°F - anything more than this and the risk of pathogen contamination increases. So, you will need a refrigerator, freezer, or any cold area where you can maintain this temperature for as long as the meat is being cured and stored.

Tips to Remember

The time required to cure the meat depends on the bone and fat in the meat and its thickness. For instance, thin cuts of meat can be cured quickly, while thicker cuts take longer. You can add a variety of herbs, spices, and other ingredients to the curing mixture.

However, do this only after you get the hang of the basic curing process and have understood the recipes well.

Whenever you place any meat in the refrigerator for curing, ensure you label the container with the date clearly. It is easy to forget when you might have placed a specific batch in the fridge.

The temperature in the refrigerator should be between 36-40°F for best results and safety.

If the meat is too salty after curing, soak it or boil it in water to get rid of the excess salt. You can reduce the curing time if the meat becomes too salty on the first attempt.

It's important to understand that cured meat is still raw. So, you will need to cook it after curing before it is fit for consumption.

Chapter 7: Guidelines for Meat Preservation

An important aspect of curing and smoking meats ensures that the essential nutrients are not lost. Since the meat is not exposed to direct heat and is instead cooked at low temperatures, its nutrients are preserved. The texture and integrity of the meat are also preserved. Adding a wonderful smoky aroma simply elevates the flavor profile of the meat altogether. Smoking also helps tenderize the meat making it easier to eat. Once you follow all the different steps discussed in the following section, the meat is ready for consumption. The savory, tender, and smoky flavors of the meat will make it simply irresistible. Besides this, all harmful pathogens are killed, and the risk of the meat going bad is drastically reduced.

Before you learn about curing meats, the three aspects you need to focus on are temperature, sanitation, and storage. Meat is not cooked until its internal temperature reaches around 160°F. Don't forget to check whether the meat is fully cooked or not before you consume it. Overcooked meat is hard and tough like rubber, but undercooked meat increases the risk of food-borne illnesses. Microbial growth usually occurs in temperatures between 40-140°F.

Once the meat is ready, ensure that you store, cure, and age it at a temperature less than 40°F.

Whenever you store the meat, make sure that all the cooked products are separated from the raw ingredients. When stored close together, the juices from one container or ingredient can transfer to another, increasing the risk of contamination. All the utensils used, include the equipment and workspace, must be thoroughly sanitized and cleaned before and after each use. Now, let's look at the different steps of preserving meat.

Selecting The Meat

Before you concentrate on preparing and preserving the meat, the first step is to select the right meat. Whenever you are purchasing meat, ensure it is not discolored. If purchasing poultry, check the area under the wings, and if there are any blood clots or bruises, check for better meat options. Poultry rarely has any odor, and if there is any, don't purchase it. Red meat has a specific odor, and it usually depends on the type of meat you want to purchase. Even if it has an odor, it should never be overpowering. There should be no slimy coating on the meat, and the flesh should be springy. Here is a simple finger test you can use. Poke the flesh with your finger. If it bounces back, it is fresh. Use this simple test to check meats before purchasing.

Curing

You will need food-grade salt, curing compounds, and meat. Alternatively, you can also purchase commercially prepared cure mixes and carefully follow the instructions on the package. To preserve meat, ensure you are starting with fresh and high-quality meat. Curing is not a method to salvage any meat close to going bad or has bacterial growth. You need not age the meat before curing it because this process and smoking will tenderize the meat itself.

Food-grade salt contains no additives- especially iodine, and this is what you should be using. If the salt has any traces of impurities, the results will not be as desirable. Before you start curing the meat, ensure it has sufficient fat content. If the meat is lean, a wet cure will be better. If you are purchasing any cure mixtures, ensure it contains nitrate for dry-cured products that are not smoked, cooked, or refrigerated. If the meat needs to be cooked, smoked, or canned, use nitrate mixtures. You can use 1o z of nitrite for 100 lb. of meat, whereas you can use 3.5 oz of nitrate for 100 lb. of meat.

You need to be extra careful whenever handling nitrates and nitrites. Nitrites become toxic if you exceed the recommended limit. As a rule of thumb, always remember one gram of sodium nitrite is lethal for an adult human. To avoid any confusion, it is better to use curing mixtures instead of working with pure nitrites.

Dry Cure

Decide on whether to dry or wet cure the meat. If you are dry curing, start by trimming any excess fat but leave a few layers so the meat doesn't dry out. If the meat has a rather thick layer of fat, penetrate it with a fork so the dry cure can enter the meat easily. Take your chosen cure and hand rub this mixture all over the meat.

Place the meat in a container laid out with parchment paper. Place something heavy on top, such as weights or a cast iron pan, to ensure the meat goes deeper into the curing mixture while leaving a small gap for flow. Transfer the meat to the refrigerator for around ten days. Once it is ready, remove it from the refrigerator, rinse it with water, and now the meat is ready for smoking.

If you are curious about making a dry rub, you can add salt, curing salt, sugar, and any spice you want to use. For instance, you can add cumin, black pepper, paprika, dry mustard, onion powder, cloves, and even Bay leaves to the rub.

Wet Cure

If you want, you have the option of wet curing the meat. It essentially means the meat will be immersed in a salt water-based liquid or brine. As a rule of thumb, the meat needs to stay in the brine solution for 12 hours per pound of weight. If the meat weighs 4 pounds, it needs to stay in the brine for 48 hours. The meats ideal for brining are the ones that tend to lose moisture during the cooking process, such as lean cuts of pork and beef.

To start brining, once again, it's important to trim any excess fat, especially the dangling bits. Place the meat in a brining bag or a sealable container that is big enough to hold the meat and the brine. The container shouldn't be filled to the brim, and there should be some space for movement. If you are using premixed brine, follow the instructions when mixing the brine cure with water. If not, you can make the brine at home.

The simplest brine recipe calls for 4 cups of water mixed with 1 cup of food-grade salt and ¼ cup of sugar. Increase the proportions based on the portions you will need. Start by heating two cups of water with salt and sugar. Once the ingredients dissolve, remove them from heat. Let this mixture come to room temperature and add the rest of the water. Place this brine mixture in the refrigerator to chill until needed. Other ingredients that can be added to the wet cure are apple cider, fresh citrus, and herbs, honey, vegetables, ginger, etc. If the mixture has at least 20% salinity, it will prevent the growth of microbes.

Let us get back to brining the meat. While the meat is stored in the refrigerator, keep turning it in the brine daily to ensure it is evenly cured. Whenever you are ready to remove the meat from the refrigerator, take it out and rinse it with water until the excess salt has washed away. The meat must be patted dry before it can be smoked. If you don't want to smoke it immediately, store it in the refrigerator until ready by wrapping it in cheesecloth.

Smoking

Now that the meat is cured, it's time to smoke it. Whether or not you have a smokehouse or use a backyard smoker, the heat, airflow, and moisture need to be well balanced. While doing this, pay specific attention to the internal temperature of the meat you are smoking. Smoking does not work as an effective preservation technique if the meat is not cooked properly. So, the first condition is that the meat should be thoroughly cooked. As explained, between the temperatures of 40-140°F, meats are at a higher risk of attracting pathogens.

The ideal internal temperature of fresh beef is between 145-170°F, depending on whether you like it rare, medium, or well done. This range is applicable for fresh lamb and veal. For ground meat and meat mixtures of turkey and chicken, the internal cooking temperature must be 165°F. If the ground meat or meat mixtures are made of pork, veal, and beef, the internal temperature must be 160°F. The ideal internal temperature for a whole chicken, turkey, duck, and goose is 180°F. For pork, the ideal internal temperature to ensure cooking is between 169-170°F.

Once the meats have reached their desired internal temperature, cool them quickly to 40°F. After this, keep it refrigerated. Try to reduce handling cooked meats if they are meant for storage.

Storage

Once the meat is cured and smoked, it is time to store it. You can store it for two weeks in the refrigerator and for a couple of months in the freezer. Refrigerate the meat within two hours of smoking. The best way to store meat is by wrapping it in butcher paper or plastic wrap. Butcher paper comes away easier than plastic wrap. After this, wrap it in a layer of aluminum foil and place it in the coldest part of the freezer. Store it at a steady temperature of around 40°F. If you want to consume it afterward, always heat it to an internal temperature of 160°F instead of tasting it right away. This is important for your safety.

Chapter 8: Guidelines for Game Preservation

Some might hunt for sport while others hunt to feed their families. If you don't want to consume game meat immediately, learning to preserve it is important. From field dressing the animals to transporting and preserving them, you need to pay attention to different aspects of this process. If you're not careful, this simply increases the risk of pathogen contamination, which can harm your health.

The most important aspect of preserving game meat is to regulate its temperature. Bacteria and other pathogens are present everywhere. Temperature plays a crucial role in their ability to survive. The most common temperature range for bacterial growth is between 40-140°F. If the temperature is less than 40°F, it is too cold for bacteria to grow. This is the reason for using a refrigerator or freezer while preserving game.

Once the game meat is ready, it must be stored in a freezer at 0°F and will last for almost a year. You must remember to cook game meat to its ideal internal temperature to preserve it. Once this temperature is reached, the bacteria in it are destroyed, which prevents food-borne illnesses. Once the meat is cooked, it needs to be cooled down rather rapidly before refrigeration. Now that you are aware of the different temperatures to pay attention to, it's time to start processing and preserving the wild game.

Aging

Game meat is usually tougher than regular meat obtained from domestic animals. Wild animals are more active and exercise for longer periods while foraging for food, escaping predators, and their surviving in general. The tenderness of the meat is associated with the location of the muscle and the age of the animal. Healthy and young animals have the most tender meat. The condition of the animal before slaughter also affects the quality of the meat. For instance, if the animal was running a long distance before it was killed, the meat tends to be sticky, gummy in texture, and darker. The energy stored in the muscle of these animals is higher, and this increases their muscle pH. As there is an increase in pH, the meat quality reduces while increasing the risk of bacterial growth.

This is one reason why it was suggested that game meat must be aged first. Aging is a simple process that tenderizes the meat while enhancing its flavor. In aging, the carcass or the meat cuts are placed in an environment with controlled temperatures and humidity levels for several days. When this happens, the enzymes present in the meat start breaking down, and the complex proteins become simplified.

If the meat doesn't have much fat, you don't have to age it, or it will dry out. If you are directly cooking the game meat by stewing, braising, or roasting, you don't have to age it because these processes will tenderize the meat. To age the meat, you will need to place it under a temperature of 40°F for up to 7 days to improve its tenderness. Pay specific attention to this temperature range. If it is above this range, it increases the risk of pathogen contamination. You can speed up this process by increasing the temperature, but this increases the risk of contamination.

Curing

You can either carve the carcass on your own or get a butcher to do it. Once the meat is ready, it's time to start curing. You can cure it with a dry rub, place it in a brine mix, or inject it with brine. These are the three methods of curing you were introduced to in the previous chapter. You can add salt, salt brine, sugar, spices, and any other ingredients you want for curing.

Once again, pay attention to the temperature at which you are doing all of this. Whether or not you are making dry curing mix at home or purchasing a readymade one, coat the meat thoroughly with it. To opt for a wet cure, you can place it in the brine solution. Injecting is rarely recommended for home curing operations. For fattier cuts of meat, choose a dry rub, while the leaner ones do well with wet curing. Once you've applied the mix to the meat, place refrigerate it at a controlled temperature of less than 40°F. As a rule of thumb, you will need to cure the meat for seven days per inch of thickness. If the meat is about 2 inches thick, it will need to cure for 14-days.

Smoking

Once you have cured the meat, it is time to smoke it. The ideal wood types to smoke game meats are hickory, oak, maple, pecan, and even mesquite in moderation. While smoking meat, especially the larger cuts or large game, consider its size and dimensions. This makes all the difference. The ideal temperature of the smoker must be maintained between 225-300°F and cook the meat until it reaches an internal temperature of 165°F. This process can take 8 hours or even longer. The time for smoking depends on the size and thickness of the meat. Once the meat is smoked, it is time to store it.

Storage

After the meat is smoked, cool it and wrap it in butcher paper and aluminum foil. Transfer it immediately into the freezer. Store it at a temperature of 0°F. The shelf life of the meat depends on the storage temperature. Don't transfer warm meat into the freezer and wait until it cools down. Also, air is your enemy while preserving meat. Whenever you store any meat in the freezer, ensure you wrap it in butcher or freezer paper or place it in Ziploc bags. You need to do this to avoid freezer burns. The idea is to preserve the meat without letting it come into direct contact with the cold air in the freezer. This is especially true for meats that will stay in the freezer for prolonged periods. One piece of equipment you can consider investing in, provided you are interested in curing and smoking regularly, is a vacuum sealer. It helps suck out any air from the bag or container used for securing and storing meats.

Chapter 9: Preserving Your Fish

One of the oldest ways to enjoy and preserve fish is by smoking them over the flame. The wonderful smoky aroma of the wood coupled with the delicate meat of freshly caught fish is quite brilliant. In this chapter, let's look at the simple steps you should follow for preserving fish at home.

Selecting the Fish

For preserving fish, starting with fresh catch is always the best. Compared to factory-farmed variants available on the market these days, fish caught in the wild is always better. The fresher the fish, the better the result produced. If you are lucky enough to get your hands on some freshly caught fish, try to keep it alive for as long as you possibly can. After this, thoroughly clean the fish and chill it so it doesn't go bad. This is especially true during warmer months when the temperature starts increasing. In such conditions, fish tends to go bad quite quickly. Don't forget to carefully store the cleaned fish and place it in an ice cooler. As a rule of thumb, you need two pounds of ice per pound of fish.

Fatty fish can absorb a smokier flavor. So, any naturally fatty fish such as trout and salmon are good options. You can either use the whole fish or parts of it for smoking. Usually, fillets with the skin are the ideal choice for smoking. It's important to consider the wood you will be using. Depending on your preference, you can choose any wood of your choice. Usually, alder is used for smoking salmon. However, any other wood, such as oak and mesquite, works well too.

Preparing the Brine

If you are making the brine at home, you need to add 2.23 lb. of salt to one gallon of water; the concentration or the strength of the brine used for soaking fish matters a lot. As a rule of thumb, dissolve one cup of salt in seven cups of water per 2-3 pounds of fish. You can always use a commercially available brine mixture. Simply follow the instructions on the packing if using a store-bought mix. To make the brine at home, combine the salt and water over low heat until the salt is fully dissolved. If the brining process takes less than 4 hours, then the ideal temperature of the brine should be less than 60°f. If it takes longer, the temperature shouldn't be higher than 38°F.

Once you have prepared the brine, it is time to make a dry rub. This step is entirely optional. Using a dry rub will further enhance the flavor of the cured fish. A simple dry rub is a Cajun spice mix that includes various spices that lend a mellow kick and flavor to the preserved fish.

Preparing the Fish

If you are using fish purchased from the market, you don't have to do anything here. You simply need to keep it on ice or place it in the fridge until you can use it. But if you are using freshly caught fish, you need to clean and prepare it. Remove the scales by scraping the dull edge of the knife against the grain of the scales. The next step is to remove the head, tail, and face. Rinse the body cavity, remove all the tissue and blood present inside. Once it's clean, cut fillets from the fish. Alternatively, you can also use the whole fish after thoroughly cleaning its body cavity.

Place It in the Brine and Rinse

Thin pieces of fish are about ½-inch thick at their thickest point and should be soaked for a maximum of ten minutes in brine. In comparison, fish over ½-inch thickness need around 30-40 minutes of soaking time. This is an important process and keeps the fish fully submerged for the desired duration. If you are placing the brine in the fridge to maintain the desired temperature, don't forget to cover it with plastic wrap. This ensures the smell of the fish does not mix with everything else in the refrigerator. Fish is quite light, and fillets are even lighter. They tend to float to the top of the bowl. To prevent this, place another bowl on top to ensure they stay submerged. The bowl holding the fish and brine shouldn't be too tightly packed. There must be room for the fish to circulate instead of getting cramped up.

After patiently waiting for the fish to soak in brine, it is time to prepare it. Remove it from the brine bath, rinse it under cool water, and dry it. The simplest and efficient way to do this is by patting them dry using paper towels. Alternatively, use grease racks and place the fish on them. Wait for around 2-3 hours or until a shiny skin or pellicle has formed on the fish. This ensures the natural juices from the fish are not lost during the smoking process. Once the fish is dry, it's time to apply the dry rub. This is entirely up to you. If you don't feel like adding any spice rub, skip the step. Before you apply the spice rub, don't forget to coat the fish lightly with a layer of butter, so the spice rub sticks to the fish evenly.

Smoke the fish

While smoking the fish, the ideal temperature should be less than 150 °F. Maintain this temperature for the initial 1-2 hours of smoking. After 2 hours, turn the heat up to 200°F and continue smoking. The fish is thoroughly cooked once it reaches an internal temperature of 165°F. It's always better to smoke the fish at a low temperature to preserve the flavor and texture. To keep the grates of the smoker clean and don't want the fish to stick to it, use aluminum foil. Place the fillets or fish on the aluminum foil with the skin side up while smoking it. If you are using skinless fillets, use a solid surface such as a wooden plank to ensure the fillets don't fall into the smoker. To regulate the smoker's temperature, especially if it tends to heat beyond 200°F, put some ice in a pan and place it inside the smoker.

Enjoy the Fish!

Once the fish is brined and smoked, it is time to enjoy it! Serve it with some baked potatoes or fries for a classic fish and chips meal. It also pairs well with crusty bread and butter, salad, and some flavored rice! If you don't want to eat it immediately, you can store it for later. To do this, wrap the smoked fish in foil or wax paper. When placed in the refrigerator, it can stay for up to 10 days. To prolong its life, you can place it in the freezer.

Chapter 10: Preserving Your Poultry

Nothing compares to the wonderful aroma and taste of smoked or cured poultry such as smoked duck or cured chicken. The salt, sugar, and nitrites present in the curing mix cure the poultry while preserving its flavor. The nitrites in the cure help retain the pinkish hue of the meat and prevent the growth of pathogens. Once you cure the meat, it can be refrigerated for up to 2 weeks. A point to remember with poultry, any uncured smoked meats should be stored for the same duration as any other regular cooked meat. In this chapter, let's look at all the different steps you can follow for preserving poultry.

Select Good Quality Poultry

As with other types of meat, starting with fresh and high-quality poultry is a must. Using good-quality ingredients makes all the difference if you want good results. For instance, choose grade-A poultry, considered the best available on the market, and use it within an hour of slaughter.

Prepare the Brine Solution

As you have learned by now, you can either make the brine solution at home or purchase a readymade mix. To make a brine solution at home for poultry, for one gallon of water, you must add 1.6 ounces of saltpeter, 0.9 lb. of non-iodized salt, and 2.4 ounces of brown or white sugar. Ensure the temperature of this mixture is 45-50°F. You can use a sodium chloride Salometer to measure the salt levels and temperature of the brine. Thoroughly mix the solution and make sure all the ingredients have dissolved completely.

A commercially prepared mixture contains the correct proportions of salt, sugar, and nitrites. This is a faster and easier procedure. If you are using a commercially prepared mixture, dissolve 1 lb. of cure mixture into a gallon of water or carefully follow the brining directions given on the packaging.

Inject the Brine

As opposed to other meats, poultry is usually injected with brine then soaked in it to hydrate the meat instead of just soaking in it. However, birds that weigh less than 3 lb., such as quails or similarly small birds, need not be brine injected and can just soak in the brine directly.

Now that the brine mix is ready, you can start injecting it into the bird. You need to inject a measurement of brine solution equivalent to 10% of the carcass's total weight. For instance, if a turkey weighs 15 lb., it needs 1.5 lb. of brine. This step is crucial because you must ensure the brine is equally distributed within the carcass. While injecting brine, you need to concentrate on different areas and not just go about randomly stabbing the carcass. While brining birds that weigh around 3-9 lb., such as capons, broilers, and pheasants, brine must be injected in three places. The birds are injected in each half of the breast, two sites on the thighs, and one on each of its drumsticks. About 60% of the brine must be injected into the breast region, 30% into the thighs, and rest into the drumsticks. Birds that weigh over 10 lb., such as turkeys, are injected into five sites. Larger birds follow the same injecting sites as smaller birds, namely, the breasts, the thighs, and the drumsticks. And you must inject the larger bird in either side of its back and once in each wing. About 50% of the brine must be injected into the breast for large birds, 25% into the thighs, 10% each into the drumsticks and wings, and the rest into the back.

Let the Poultry Soak

Now, this step is all about patience. Once you have injected your poultry, place it in either a plastic or stainless-steel container (food-use quality). Ensure the remaining brine is at a temperature between 34-36°F and cover the bird with it. You will need around a 5-10-gallon mixture of brine for curing two turkeys or over three broilers. You will need sufficient brine so the bird is immersed in it. Place the poultry inside an insulated ice chest to retain the desired brine temperature. You can always add more ice to maintain the temperature. However, remember the proportions of the cure must be maintained as more ice is added. As mentioned, quail and other similarly small birds need not be injected with brine and can be directly placed in the brine solution. Small birds need to stay immersed in brine for 4-6 hours, while small broilers that are not injected need about 4-8 hours in brine. Broilers, pheasants, capons, and turkeys weighing less than 10 lb. need to stay in the brine for 24-36 hours, while bigger birds need 48-72 hours.

Draining and Netting

Once the poultry is cured for the desired time, remove it from the brine solution, drain it, and let it dry for 15 minutes. There should be no extra brine left in its body cavity. If you have a conventional smokehouse, place them on stockinette and have them hanging breast-side down. If you are using a backyard barbecue smoker or cooker, you need not do this. Instead, tie the bird's legs together using a piece of string or twine, tuck its wings towards the breast, and let it dry out. This helps the bird retain its shape even after cooking.

Smoking

Once the bird is almost dry, place it in the backyard smoker or the smokehouse. The ideal temperature for this step is around 170°F. Smoke can be applied only when the bird is completely dry. If you don't let the bird dry out completely, the carcass will have a streaked look after being smoked. Don't be in a rush and slowly cook the bird on a low fire while generating plenty of smoke. While smoking, keep the bird as far away from the heat source as you possibly can. The best woods for smoking poultry are pecan, green hickory, oak, mesquite, and other fruitwoods.

The time taken for smoking poultry depends on the thickness of the meat, whether it is deboned or not, and its fat content. Other factors are the external weather conditions and the insulation on the smoker. The smoker and the fuel it uses also influence the cooking time. Besides this, another factor you need to consider is whether the meat was at room temperature before you started smoking it or not. It usually takes 4-5 hours to smoke a whole turkey, whereas a whole chicken only takes 2-3 hours.

Complete the Cooking Process

When the bird has reached the desired color, increase the temperature to 200-225°F to complete the cooking process. Check the internal temperature of the bird. It is not fully cooked unless it reaches an internal temperature of 162-165°F in the fleshy muscles. You can also check whether the bird is fully cooked or not by twisting the leg quarter. If it moves freely, the bird is fully cooked. Don't be alarmed if the bird's size shrinks by 20% or so during the cooking process. Brining and smoking remove the salt and moisture present on the inside resulting in the size reduction.

Storage

Once you have followed all the steps for brining and smoking, it's time to store the cured poultry. You don't have to cook it any further, and it can stay refrigerated for up to two weeks. This is the same timeframe applicable to other cured meats as well. To store it for longer than 2-weeks, ensure it is kept in the freezer at 0°F. If the poultry is packed, cured, smoked, and stored properly, it can retain its quality and flavor for up to one year.

Chapter 11: Poultry and Meat Recipes

Smoked Chicken

Ingredients:

<u>If using brine:</u>

- 8 cups water
- 1 whole chicken (2 pounds), rinsed
- ½ cup Fette Sau dry rub

<u>If using dry rub:</u>

- ½ cup Fette Sau dry rub or as much as required
- 1 whole chicken (2 pounds)

<u>For Fette Sau dry rub:</u>

- 6 tablespoons packed dark brown sugar
- ¼ cup ground espresso beans
- 1 tablespoon garlic powder
- ½ tablespoon ground cumin
- ¼ cup kosher salt

- 1 tablespoon freshly ground black pepper
- ½ tablespoon ground cinnamon
- ½ tablespoon cayenne pepper

Directions:

1. To make Fette Sau dry rub: Mix sugar, espresso beans, garlic powder, cumin, salt, black pepper, cinnamon, and cayenne pepper in an airtight container. Close the lid and shake the container to mix well. Use as much as required and store the remaining.

2. Place the spice container in a cool area. It can last for two months.

3. Dry the chicken well with paper towels. You should dry it inside as well as on the outside.

4. If you use brine for the chicken, combine water and Fette Sau dry rub in a stockpot.

5. Place the pot over high heat. Stir until all the sugar and salt dissolve completely. Turn off the heat and let the brine cool completely.

6. Pour the brine into a non-reactive container and chill for 3 - 4 hours.

7. Place chicken in the chilled brine and place the container in the refrigerator. Let it chill for 4 - 8 hours.

8. Have a wire rack placed on a rimmed baking sheet.

9. Take the chicken out from the brine and dry it with paper towels. Place it on the wire rack. Discard the brine.

10. Now place the chicken on the rack along with the baking sheet in the refrigerator. After 6 hours, take it out from the refrigerator for smoking.

11. If you are using only a dry rub, keep the chicken on a rimmed baking sheet. Sprinkle the dry rub all over the chicken. Use only as much rub as required, suiting your taste.

12. Set up your smoker and preheat it to 225°F. Place the chicken into the smoker and smoke the chicken. Add wood chunks or wood chips as and when required. See that the temperature of the smoker is maintained between 200°F and 225°F. Follow the manufacturer's instructions for adding wood chips.

13. The time for smoking chicken is approximately 45 minutes per pound. So roughly for 1 – 1-½ hours. When done with the smoking, the internal temperature in the center of the chicken leg should show 165°F when checked with an instant-read thermometer.

14. Place the chicken on your cutting board. Give it a rest for about 10 – 15 minutes.

15. You can now cut, shred or chop the chicken and use it. For a crisp skin, you can roast the whole chicken in an indirect method on the grill. Cover the grill while roasting. You can also crisp it up in an oven at 450°F.

Smoked Chicken Wings

Ingredients:

- 1 ½ pounds chicken wings, separated into drums and flats
- ¾ tablespoon baking powder or cornstarch
- 1 tablespoon kosher salt
- ½ cup Franks Red hot sauce
- 2 tablespoons butter
- 1 ½ tablespoons poultry rub
- 9 ounces IPA beer
- 10 tablespoons brown sugar
- 2 tablespoons butter

Directions:

1. Place the wings into a Ziploc bag. Add ½ tablespoon rub, 2 tablespoons of brown sugar, and salt in the bag—drizzle 6 ounces of beer over the chicken.

2. After sealing the bag, turn the bag around a few times so that chicken is well coated with the marinade. Keep the bag in the refrigerator for 12 - 15 hours.

3. Take out the wings from the bag, dry the wings by patting them with paper towels, and then transfer them to a bowl. Sprinkle cornstarch and remaining rub over the wings.

4. Place the wings on a baking sheet lined with aluminum foil.

5. Set up your smoker and preheat it to 150°F. Place the wings in the smoker on the grill grate, and smoke them for 30 minutes. Add wood chunks or wood chips when required (follow the manufacturer's instructions on how to

use the wood chips). See that the temperature of the smoker is maintained between 145°F and 150°F.

6. Next, set the temperature of the smoker to 350°F and cook for another 40 – 45 minutes.

7. Meanwhile, combine red-hot sauce, butter, remaining brown sugar, and remaining beer in a small saucepan. Cook the sauce mixture until it is reduced to half of its original quantity.

8. Take out the wings from the grill and add them into a large serving bowl. Drizzle sauce mixture on top and toss well.

9. Serve.

Smoked BBQ Korean Chicken Wings

Ingredients:

For brine:

- 1 quart water
- ¼ cup sugar
- ¼ head garlic, sliced
- 5 black peppercorns
- ½ cup sea salt
- ½ lemon
- 2 sprigs thyme

For wings:

- 1 tablespoon olive oil
- 1 ½ pounds chicken wings

For sauce:

- ¼ cup gochujang paste
- 3 tablespoons honey
- 1 tablespoon lime juice
- 2 tablespoons butter, melted
- ½ tablespoon grated ginger
- ¼ cup soy sauce
- 1 tablespoon rice wine vinegar
- 1 tablespoon sesame oil
- 2 cloves garlic, minced

To garnish:

- 1 green onion, thinly sliced
- 3 tablespoons sesame seeds

Directions:

1. Pour water into a saucepan. Add salt and sugar and heat over high flame. Stir often until sugar and salt dissolve completely.

2. When the brine solution begins to boil, turn off the heat. Add lemon, thyme, garlic, and peppercorns and stir.

3. Let it cool completely. Transfer the brine into a container. Drop the chicken wings into the container. Cover the container and keep it refrigerated for 4 – 8 hours.

4. Take out the chicken wings from the brine and dry them by patting them with paper towels.

5. Brush oil over the wings.

6. Set up your smoker and preheat it to 275°F. Place the chicken in the smoker on the grill grate, and smoke the chicken wings for 30 minutes. Add wood chunks or wood chips when required (follow the manufacturer's instructions on how to use the wood chips). See that the temperature of the smoker is maintained between 250°F and 275°F.

7. Next, set the smoker's temperature to 375°F and cook for an additional 50 – 60 minutes or until the internal temperature of the chicken shows around 170°F to 175°F.

8. Meanwhile, make the sauce: For this, combine gochujang paste, honey, lime juice, butter, ginger, soy sauce, vinegar, sesame oil, and garlic in a saucepan. Heat the mixture over medium flame and let it come to a simmer. Turn off the heat.

9. Add wings into the sauce. Toss well. Add green onion and sesame seeds and toss well.

10. Serve immediately.

Smoked Herb Chicken

Ingredients:

- 1 whole chicken (about 2 pounds), rinsed
- ½ chopped tablespoon fresh parsley
- ½ tablespoon chopped fresh basil
- ½ tablespoon chopped fresh oregano
- ½ tablespoon chopped fresh chives
- 2 tablespoons butter, chopped into pieces

Directions:

1. Dry the chicken well with paper towels. Dry it inside as well as on the outside.

2. Loosen the skin all around the breast of the chicken. Place the pieces of butter in different places below the skin.

3. Mix parsley, basil, oregano, and chives in a bowl. Place half the herbs below the skin and stuff the remaining inside the chicken.

4. Set up your smoker and preheat it to 200°F. Insert the chicken in the smoker and smoke the chicken. Add wood chunks or wood chips as and when required. (Follow the manufacturer's instructions on how to use the wood chips). See to it that the temperature of the smoker is maintained between 150°F and 200°F.

5. The time for smoking chicken is approximately 45 minutes per pound. So roughly after 1 – 1-½ hours, the chicken should be smoked. When you are done with the smoking, the internal temperature in the center of the chicken leg should show 165°F when checked with an instant-read thermometer.

6. Place the chicken on your cutting board. Let it rest for about 10 – 15 minutes.

Smoked Pulled Chicken

Ingredients:

- 2 ½ pounds chicken thighs, boneless
- 2 – 3 tablespoons BBQ rub
- ¼ cup BBQ sauce

For brine:

- ½ cup kosher salt
- 1 quart water

To make sandwiches: Optional

- Red onion slices
- 4 seeded or brioche buns
- Any other toppings of your choice

Directions:

1. Combine salt and water in a brining bucket. Once the salt is completely dissolved, add chicken thighs into the bucket.

2. Transfer the brining bucket into the refrigerator. Let it chill for an hour.

3. Dry the chicken well with paper towels.

4. Set up your smoker and preheat it to 225°F. Place the chicken thighs in the smoker, on the racks, leaving a gap between the thighs and smoke the chicken thighs. Add wood chunks or wood chips as and when required. (Follow the manufacturer's instructions on how to use the wood chips). See to it that the temperature of the smoker is maintained between 200°F and 225°F.

5. When you are done with the smoking, the internal temperature in the center of the chicken thigh should show 165°F when checked with an instant-read thermometer.

6. Place the chicken on your cutting board. Cover loosely with aluminum foil. Let it rest for 10 - 15 minutes.

7. Shred the meat with a pair of forks. You can now use the chicken for salads or soups, etc.

8. For BBQ flavored chicken sandwiches: Place the shredded chicken in a bowl. Pour BBQ sauce over it and toss well.

9. Serve over buns with onion slices and any other toppings of your choice.

Smoked Chicken Salad

Ingredients:

- 2 – 3 cups smoked, shredded chicken
- 2 oranges, peeled, separated into segments, deseeded, chopped
- 2 cooked beetroots, cooled, peeled, chopped into cubes
- Chopped cilantro

<u>For dressing:</u>

- 1 teaspoon honey
- 1 tablespoon yogurt or sour cream
- ¼ teaspoon Dijon mustard

Directions:

1. For smoked chicken, follow the recipe for smoked herb chicken, or smoked pulled chicken, or smoked chicken in this chapter.

2. Combine chicken, oranges, beets, and cilantro in a bowl.

3. To make the dressing: Combine honey, yogurt, and Dijon mustard in a bowl. Pour dressing over the salad. Toss well and serve.

Brunswick Stew

Ingredients:

- 2 pounds smoked meat of your choice
- 1-pound smoked chicken
- 6 large potatoes, peeled, cut into cubes
- 2 pounds corn kernels
- 2 tablespoons cider vinegar
- 2 cans chopped tomatoes
- 2 onions, chopped into chunks
- 4 tablespoons Worcestershire sauce
- 2 tablespoons sugar
- 2 tablespoons tomato paste
- Pepper to taste
- Salt to taste

<u>To serve:</u> Optional

- Cooked rice
- Crusty bread

Directions:

1. Set up your oven and preheat it to 260°F.

2. Place half the potatoes into the food processor bowl and process until smooth. Transfer into a bowl.

3. Add half the corn into the food processor bowl and process until smooth. Transfer into the bowl of potatoes and mix.

4. Place onions into the food processor bowl and process until smooth. Transfer into the bowl of potatoes and corn and mix until smooth.

5. Place all the meat, remaining chopped potatoes, remaining corn, vinegar, tomatoes, pepper, Worcestershire sauce, sugar, tomato paste, and salt into a Dutch oven.

6. Pour blended potato mixture into the pot and stir. Close the lid. Place the Dutch oven in the oven and cook for 5 - 6 hours.

7. Check on it after 4 hours. If the stew is looking very dry, add some water. If it is watery, uncover and cook until the desired thickness is achieved.

8. Serve over rice or with crusty bread.

Smoked Turkey

Ingredients:

- 10 -12 pounds turkey

For brine:

- 1 cup kosher salt
- ½ bottle white wine
- 2-3 navel oranges
- 2 large onions, chopped
- 3 bay leaves
- ½ bottle red wine
- 2 cups chicken broth
- 2 tablespoons whole peppercorns
- 2 tablespoons whole cloves
- Cloves from ½ head garlic, peeled, chopped

After brine:

- Vegetable oil, as needed
- Freshly ground pepper to taste
- 3 – 4 cloves garlic, chopped
- 3-4 tablespoons soy sauce
- ½ apple, cored, quartered
- 1/8 large onion, chopped

Directions:

1. Add salt and about 2 quarts of boiling water into a large stockpot or brining bucket. Add red wine, white wine, and broth. Juice the oranges and add the juice into the brining bucket. Add the peels of the oranges, garlic, onion,

peppercorns, bay leaves, and cloves. Stir the brine solution until the salt dissolves completely.

2. Place the turkey in the brine breast side down in the bucket.

3. Place the turkey with brine in the refrigerator for at least 12 hours. The turkey may turn purple in color, but that is nothing to worry about. In fact, it will taste even better.

4. Remove the turkey from the brine and pat it dry with paper towels. Rub oil over the turkey. Brush soy sauce all over the turkey and rub it well into it.

5. Sprinkle a generous amount of pepper all over the turkey. Keep the turkey on the rack in a turkey pan.

6. Stuff the inner hollow cavity (the cavity should be cleaned, so remove everything from the cavity beforehand) with onions, garlic, and apple.

7. Take two large sheets of foil and fold one of its ends into a point. Place this point in between the legs of the turkey.

8. Brush oil on the foil that will touch the turkey while covering it. Fold the foil over the body of the turkey.

9. Set up your smoker and preheat it to 500°F. Place lava stone under the grill grates.

10. Place the turkey in the smoker along with the pan on the grill grate. Close the lid and smoke the turkey for about 30 minutes. Add wood chunks or wood chips as and when required (follow the manufacturer's instructions on how to use the wood chips). See that the temperature of the smoker is maintained between 450°F and 500°F.

11. Remove the turkey from the grill and lower the temperature of the grill to 325° F.

12. Place a meat thermometer in the thickest part of the meat. Place the turkey back in the grill. Cover and cook until the temperature of the thermometer reads 165° F in the thickest part of the breast area.

13. Remove the turkey from the grill and let it sit for 45 minutes (do not uncover the turkey).

14. Uncover the turkey.

15. Cut into slices and serve.

Smoked Chicken Breast

Ingredients:

- 3 tablespoons table salt or 5 tablespoons kosher salt
- 1 quart water
- 1 ½ teaspoons minced garlic
- 1 - 2 sprigs of fresh thyme
- ¼ cup brown sugar
- 1 chicken breast, bone-in, skin-on
- 2 thin lemon slices
- 1 - 2 sprigs of fresh rosemary

Directions:

1. To make the brine: Combine water, brown sugar, and salt in a container.

2. Stir until sugar and salt dissolve completely.

3. Insert the chicken into the brine. Make sure the chicken is immersed in the water. Place something heavy on the chicken, if necessary, to keep it submerged.

4. Keep the container in the refrigerator for 7 - 9 hours. Take it out of the refrigerator about 30 minutes before smoking.

5. Set up your smoker and preheat it to 225°F for 15 minutes.

6. Take out the chicken from the brine and dry it with paper towels. Discard the brine.

7. Rub the chicken with garlic. The skin of the chicken is to be loosened.

8. Place the lemon slices, garlic, and herbs between the skin and meat.

9. Place the chicken on the grill and smoke the chicken. Add wood chunks or wood chips as and when required. See that the temperature of the smoker is maintained between 200°F and 225°F. Follow the manufacturer's instructions for adding wood chips.

10. When done with the smoking, the internal temperature in the center of the chicken breast should show 160°F when checked with an instant-read thermometer.

11. Place the chicken on your cutting board. Let it rest for about 10 – 15 minutes.

12. Slice or shred and serve.

Baked Potato and Smoked Chicken Casserole

Ingredients:

- 2 ¼ pounds red potatoes, cubed
- ½ pound pulled smoked chicken
- 4 slices bacon, cooked until crisp, crumbled
- ¾ cup sour cream
- Red pepper sauce to taste
- 1 ½ tablespoons olive oil
- ¼ teaspoon freshly ground pepper
- 6 tablespoons BBQ sauce
- 4 ounces shredded sharp cheddar cheese
- ¼ cup chopped green onions
- Salt to taste

Directions:

1. Preheat the oven to 400°F.

2. Grease a baking dish with some cooking spray and prepare the potatoes for baking.

3. Place potatoes in a bowl. Drizzle oil over them. Sprinkle salt and pepper and toss well.

4. Spread the potatoes in the baking dish.

5. Place the baking dish in the oven and bake for 20 minutes. Stir and continue baking for another 20 minutes or until the potatoes are crisp on the outside and fork-tender inside.

6. Combine smoked chicken and BBQ sauce in a bowl and spread over the potatoes.

7. Scatter bacon and cheese on top.

8. Put the baking dish back into the oven and bake for 10 to 12 minutes or until the cheese melts and is bubbling.

9. Drizzle sour cream on top. Scatter green onions on top. Drizzle some hot pepper sauce to taste and serve.

Penne with Smoked Chicken and Mascarpone

Ingredients:

- ½ pound penne pasta
- 1 tablespoon sherry vinegar
- 4 ounces young green beans, cut into 1 ½ inch pieces, blanched for about 2 minutes
- 1 shallot, thinly sliced
- Crushed red pepper to taste
- 1 tablespoon minced parsley
- ¼ cup mascarpone cheese
- ½ tablespoon extra-virgin olive oil
- 4 ounces zucchini, cut into 1 ½ x 1/3-inch sticks
- ½ pound boneless smoked chicken breast, remove skin and fat, shredded
- Salt to taste

Directions:

1. Cook pasta according to the directions on the package of pasta.

2. Retain about ¼ - ½ cup of the cooking liquid and drain off the rest. Set the pasta aside.

3. Cook mascarpone cheese and vinegar in a stainless-steel saucepan on low heat. Once the mixture melts, turn off the heat and keep it covered.

4. Place a nonstick skillet over medium heat. Pour oil into it and let it heat up. Once the oil is hot, add the zucchini and green beans and cook until tender.

5. Add shallots and cook until light brown.

6. Stir in smoked chicken, salt, and crushed red pepper and heat thoroughly. Transfer into a large bowl.

7. Add cooked pasta into the bowl of chicken. Add mascarpone cheese sauce mixture and retained pasta cooked liquid and toss well.

8. Garnish with parsley and serve.

Chopped Salad with Smoked Brisket

Ingredients:

For dressing:

- 2 tablespoons red wine vinegar
- Salt to taste
- ¼ cup extra-virgin olive oil
- ½ tablespoon minced garlic
- Freshly cracked pepper to taste

For salad:

- 3 cups chopped lacinato kale or Romaine lettuce
- ½ cup halved cherry tomatoes
- ½ red bell pepper, chopped
- 2 – 3 cups pulled or chopped smoked brisket (refer to smoked brisket recipe in this chapter)
- ½ cup chopped red cabbage
- ½ small red onion, thinly sliced
- ½ cucumber, peeled, sliced

Directions:

1. To make the dressing: Place garlic, vinegar, salt, and pepper in a bowl and whisk until well combined.

2. Pour oil in a thin drizzle, whisking all the time. Keep whisking until the dressing is emulsified.

3. To make the salad: Place Romaine lettuce or kale, tomatoes, bell pepper, cucumber, cabbage, and onion in a bowl and toss well.

4. Add dressing and stir until well combined.

5. Divide salad into plates. Scatter brisket on top and serve.

Cured Beef and Pickle Sandwich

Ingredients:

- 2 gherkins, cut into thin slices lengthwise
- 2 teaspoons honey mustard or medium-hot mustard or more to taste
- 4 slices of whole-wheat bread or any other bread of your choice
- ¾ cup pastrami (refer to pastrami recipe in this chapter)

Directions:

1. Smear 1 teaspoon mustard on one side of 2 of the bread slices.

2. Place pastrami and gherkin slices over the bread slices.

3. Cover with the remaining bread slices and serve.

Loaded Grilled Italian Sandwich

Ingredients:

- 2 loaves (16 ounces each) Italian bread, halved lengthwise
- 4 cloves garlic, peeled
- 2 cups roasted red bell peppers
- 12 ounces sliced provolone cheese
- 24 ounces kalamata olives, drained
- 1 cup marinated artichokes
- 2 tablespoons oil from the marinated artichokes
- 12 ounces salami slices
- 4 cups arugula

Directions:

1. Scoop out the insides of the bread halves to resemble boats. Make sure the outer part of the bread is not pinched or torn. The scooped bread can be used in another recipe that needs breadcrumbs.

2. Place olives, garlic, and oil from artichoke hearts in a blender and blend until smooth.

3. Spread the artichoke puree on the cut side of the bread halves, filling the scooped part as well. Use all the mixture.

4. Place cheese slices over the bread halves.

5. Place the salami, roasted red peppers, and arugula on the bottom halves of the loaves.

6. Close the sandwiches with the top half of the loaves.

7. Preheat the oven to 350°F.

8. Take 2 large sheets of aluminum foil. Place a sandwich on each and wrap them completely.

9. Bake for 15 – 18 minutes. Unwrap and bake for about 5 minutes.

10. Cut into 3-inch slices and serve.

Corned Beef Hash

Ingredients:

- 1 ½ tablespoons unsalted butter
- 1 ½ cups finely chopped corned beef
- 1 tablespoon chopped fresh parsley
- ½ cup chopped onion
- Salt and pepper to taste
- 1 ½ cups cooked, chopped potatoes
- Fried eggs or poached eggs to serve

Directions:

1. Place a cast-iron skillet over medium flame. Add butter and let it melt.

2. Once butter melts, add onion and cook until pink.

3. Stir in corned beef and potatoes. Now spread the beef moisture all over the pan and raise the heat to medium-high heat.

4. Press the mixture with a metal spatula, making sure not to stir. Let it cook for a few minutes.

5. Once the underside is brown, flip sides. Add more butter if required. Press the mixture once again, making sure not to stir. Let it cook until brown.

6. Turn off the heat. Add a generous amount of pepper and some parsley and stir.

7. Serve with eggs, either fried or poached.

Corned Beef Cottage Pie

Ingredients:

<u>For mashed potatoes:</u>
- ½ pound potatoes, peeled, quartered
- 1 tablespoon butter
- 3 tablespoons milk
- Salt to taste

<u>For corned beef filling:</u>
- ½ cup diced onions
- ¾ - 1 tablespoon ketchup
- 1 tablespoon chopped fresh parsley
- 1 ¼ cups finely diced corned beef
- 1 tablespoon butter
- ½ teaspoon Worcestershire sauce or to taste
- ¾ cup chicken or beef broth
- 1/8 teaspoon dried thyme
- Salt to taste
- Freshly ground pepper to taste

<u>For topping:</u>
- 2 tablespoons dried breadcrumbs or 3 tablespoons fresh breadcrumbs

Directions:

1. To make mashed potatoes: Boil potatoes in salted water until soft.

2. Combine butter and milk in a saucepan and heat over a low flame. When the butter melts, turn off the heat and mix well. Cover and keep it warm.

3. Drain off the water from the cooked potatoes and add it back into the pot.

4. Keep the pot over medium flame. Pour the milk mixture into the pot. Using a potato masher, mash the mixture, adding some more milk if required.

5. Add salt and pepper to taste. Turn off the heat. Keep the pot covered until you make the filling.

6. While you are making the filling, preheat the oven to 400°F.

7. To make the filling: Melt butter in a skillet placed over medium flame.

8. Cook onions in the butter until light golden brown. Stir in broth, ketchup, Worcestershire sauce, thyme, and parsley and cook until the broth in the pan is reduced to half of its original quantity.

9. Stir in corned beef and lower the flame. Cook until nearly dry. Add salt and pepper to taste and turn off the heat.

10. Spread the mixture into a baking dish. Spread the mashed potatoes over the meat layer.

11. The next layer will be cheese and breadcrumbs right on top.

12. Place the baking dish in the oven and bake until golden brown on top.

Pepperoni Pasta Bake

Ingredients:

- ½ pound dry pasta
- 1 small onion, diced
- 2 cloves garlic, minced
- ½ can (15 ounces can) diced tomatoes, drained
- ¼ cup grated parmesan cheese
- 1 cup marinara sauce
- 1 cup shredded mozzarella cheese, divided
- 15 – 20 pepperoni slices, halved
- ½ tablespoon olive oil
- ¼ teaspoon dried oregano

Optional toppings:

- 4 – 6 leaves fresh basil, chopped
- ¼ cup shaved parmesan

Directions:

1. Follow the directions on the package and cook the pasta in salted water. Turn off the heat. Drain off the cooking water and add the pasta back into the cooking pot.

2. While the pasta is cooking, preheat your oven to 375°F.

3. Meanwhile, pour oil into a skillet and heat over medium flame. When the oil is hot, add onion and cook until pink.

4. Stir in oregano and garlic and cook until you get a nice fragrance. Turn off the heat. Transfer this mixture into the pot of pasta. Add tomatoes, marinara sauce, parmesan

cheese, most of the mozzarella and pepperonis. Stir until well incorporated.

5. Grease a baking dish and add the pasta mixture to the baking dish. Top with retained mozzarella cheese.

6. Place the baking dish in the oven for about 20 minutes or until the cheese melts and is starting to brown.

7. Serve hot.

Pepperoni Meatloaf

Ingredients:

- 6 cups chopped pepperoni
- ½ cup sliced pepperoni or more if desired
- 2 cans (15 ounces each) tomato sauce
- 1 cup grated parmesan cheese
- 6 tablespoons dried minced onions
- 2 tablespoons garlic powder
- 1 teaspoon dried tarragon
- 2 pounds extra-lean ground beef
- 1 ½ cups cracker crumbs
- 4 eggs
- ¼ cup French fried onions
- 3 teaspoons dried oregano

Directions:

1. Preheat your oven to 350°F when you start preparing the meatloaf.

2. Place ground beef, tomato sauce, chopped pepperoni, cracker crumbs, eggs, parmesan cheese, dried minced onions, garlic powder, oregano, tarragon, and French-fried onions in a bowl and mix until well combined. Do not mix for too long, as the meat will get tough.

3. Place the mixture in a large loaf pan. Use two smaller loaf pans if you do not have a large one. The top of the loaf should be smooth. You can use a spatula to do so.

4. Place the meatloaf in the oven and bake for about an hour or until the meat is not pink anymore. When the loaf is cooked, the temperature in the middle of the meatloaf should show 160°F on a meat thermometer.

5. Now top with the pepperoni slices and continue baking for another 5 minutes.

6. Take it out from the oven and let it cool.

7. Cut into slices and serve. Store leftovers in an airtight container in the refrigerator until use. Consume within 4 – 5 days.

Smoked Pork Ribs

Ingredients:

- 2 racks of baby back ribs, trimmed
- BBQ sauce, as needed (optional)

For the rub:

- ½ tablespoon ground pepper
- 1 tablespoon Hungarian sweet paprika
- 2 tablespoons celery salt
- 2 teaspoons kosher salt
- 1 tablespoon onion powder
- 2 tablespoons garlic powder

For bath:

- 1 tablespoon brown sugar
- 2 tablespoons apple juice or cider
- 1 tablespoon apple cider vinegar
- 2 tablespoons butter, cubed

Directions:

1. Dry the ribs by patting them with paper towels.

2. To make the rub: Combine all the spices, celery salt, and kosher salt in a bowl.

3. Sprinkle the rub all over the ribs.

4. Set up your smoker and preheat it to 225°F. Place the ribs in the smoker and smoke the ribs for about 3 hours. Add wood chunks or wood chips as and when required. (Follow the manufacturer's instructions on how to use the wood chips). See that the temperature of the smoker is maintained between 200°F and 225°F.

5. Take a large sheet of foil or use two sheets of foil. Place the ribs on the foil. Top with brown sugar, apple juice, vinegar, and butter. Wrap the ribs tightly. If you are using two sheets of foil, place one rib on each foil. Divide the brown sugar, apple juice, vinegar, and butter among the ribs and place them on top. Wrap tightly.

6. Place the packets in the smoker and cook for 2 hours.

7. Without sauce: Unwrap and brush ribs with the cooked liquids. Roast for some time until crunchy, making sure to baste with the cooking liquid a few times. Let the ribs rest for 15 minutes. Cut into slices and serve.

8. With sauce: Brush some BBQ sauce over the ribs, and roast for 15 minutes. Repeat this process 3 more times (i.e., brushing ribs with BBQ sauce and roasting for 15 minutes).

9. Let the ribs rest for 15 minutes. Cut into slices and serve.

Smoked Pork Tenderloin

Ingredients:

- 12 tablespoons butter
- 4 pork tenderloins (1 pound each)

<u>For brine:</u>

- ½ cup salt
- 6 tablespoons honey
- 4 cups water

<u>For the rub:</u>

- 2 tablespoons brown sugar
- 2 teaspoons garlic powder
- 4 teaspoons kosher salt
- 1 teaspoon chili powder (optional)
- ½ tablespoon ground pepper
- 2 tablespoons paprika
- 1 tablespoon onion powder

Directions:

1. Pour water and honey into a saucepan, add the salt, and stir. Place the saucepan over medium flame. When the brine is warm, turn off the heat and let it cool completely.

2. Place pork tenderloins in a brining bucket or large stockpot. Pour the brine over the pork.

3. Place the brining bucket in the refrigerator for 8 to 10 hours.

4. Take out the pork tenderloins from the brine and dry them by patting them with paper towels.

5. Discard the silver skin from the tenderloins.

6.   Sprinkle spice rub all over the tenderloins and tie them up with a butcher string.

7.   Set up your smoker and preheat it to 180°F. Place the tenderloins in the smoker and smoke them for about 3 hours or until the internal temperature of the meat in the thickest part shows 120°F on an instant-read thermometer or meat thermometer. Add wood chunks or wood chips as and when required. (Follow the manufacturer's instructions on how to use the wood chips). See to it that the temperature of the smoker is maintained between 170°F and 180°F.

8.   Next, raise the temperature of the smoker to 400°F and cook the tenderloins until the internal temperature of the meat in the thickest part is 160°F.

9.   Once cooked, remove them from the smoker and place on your cutting board. Tent loosely with foil and let it rest for 15 minutes.

10. Cut into slices diagonally.

Smoked Pulled Pork

Ingredients:

- 3 - 4 pounds bone-in pork shoulder
- 2 tablespoons pork rub or add more to taste
- 1 tablespoon avocado oil or olive oil, or any other oil of your choice

Directions:

1. For pork rub, you can use your own favorite rub, homemade or store-bought. You can also use the rub from the recipes for smoked pork ribs or smoked pork tenderloin.

2. Rub oil all over the meat. Sprinkle rub all over and rub it well into it.

3. Set up your smoker and preheat it to 225°F. Place the meat in the smoker and smoke them for about 3 - 4 hours or until the internal temperature of the meat in the thickest part shows 160°F on an instant-read thermometer or meat thermometer. Add wood chunks or wood chips as and when required. (Follow the manufacturer's instructions on how to use the wood chips). See to it that the temperature of the smoker is maintained between 200°F and 225°F.

4. Next, wrap the meat with butcher paper and place it back in the smoker. Smoke the meat until the internal temperature of the meat shows 200°F - 205°F on the thermometer.

5. Take out the meat from the smoker and do not remove the butcher paper.

6. Wrap the meat with a layer of aluminum foil and keep it in a cooler for resting. Let it rest for 2 - 5 hours.

7. Remove the meat from its wrapping and shred the meat with a pair of forks. You can serve it over buns along with **BBQ** sauce or any other toppings of your choice like coleslaw, lettuce, cheese, tomatoes, etc.

Smoked Brisket

Ingredients:

- 14 – 16 pounds whole brisket
- 6 – 7 tablespoons BBQ rub
- 3 – 4 tablespoons garlic-infused olive oil

Directions:

1. Leave about ¼ inch of fat and trim off the remaining fat from the brisket.

2. Apply a generous amount of garlic-infused oil all over the brisket and rub it in well.

3. Set up your smoker and preheat it to 225°F. Place the brisket in a roasting pan in the smoker and smoke the brisket until the internal temperature of the meat in the thickest part shows 160°F on an instant-read thermometer or meat thermometer. The approximate timing is 1 – 1 ½ hours of smoking per pound of meat. Add wood chunks or wood chips as and when required. (Follow the manufacturer's instructions on how to use the wood chips). See to it that the temperature of the smoker is maintained between 200°F and 225°F.

4. Once the internal temperature of 160°F is reached, wrap the meat in butcher paper and keep it back in the smoker. When the internal temperature shows 200°F, take it out from the smoker.

5. Do not remove the butcher paper.

6. Wrap the meat with a layer of aluminum foil and keep it in a cooler for resting. Let it rest for 2 – 5 hours.

7. Remove the meat from its wrapping and slice it against the grain and serve.

Coffee-Rubbed Texas-Style Brisket

Ingredients:

- 2 tablespoons ground coffee
- 2 tablespoons dark brown sugar
- 4 teaspoons ancho chili powder
- 2 teaspoons onion powder
- 2 teaspoons freshly ground pepper
- 2 tablespoons kosher salt
- 4 teaspoons smoked paprika
- 2 teaspoons garlic powder
- 2 teaspoons ground cumin
- About 9 pounds flat-cut brisket (about 3 inches thick)

Directions:

1. Mix coffee, salt, and all the spices in a bowl. Rub this mixture all over the brisket.

2. Set up your smoker and preheat it to 225°F. Place the brisket in a roasting pan in the smoker and smoke the brisket until the internal temperature of the meat in the thickest part shows 160°F on an instant-read thermometer or meat thermometer. The approximate timing is 1 - 1 ½ hours of smoking per pound of meat. Add wood chunks or wood chips as and when required. (Follow the manufacturer's instructions on how to use the wood chips). See to it that the temperature of the smoker is maintained between 200°F and 225°F.

3. Once the internal temperature of 160°F is reached, wrap the meat in butcher paper and keep it back in the smoker. When the internal temperature shows 200°F, take it out from the smoker.

4. Do not remove the butcher paper.

5. Wrap the meat with a layer of aluminum foil and keep it in a cooler for resting. Let it rest for 2 – 5 hours.

6. Wrap the meat with a layer of aluminum foil and slice it against the grain.

7. Serve it along with the juices collected while smoking.

Irish Smoked Beef Brisket

Ingredients:

- 6 pounds rolled brisket
- 1 cup brown sugar
- ½ cup vegetable oil
- 4 tablespoons lemon juice
- 2 tablespoons ground black pepper
- 4 cloves garlic, crushed
- 2 teaspoons dried chili flakes
- 2 bottles Guinness
- 1 cup water
- ½ cup Worcestershire sauce
- 2 tablespoons cooking salt
- 2 tablespoons soy sauce
- 2 large onions, sliced

For sauce:

- 2 tablespoons vinegar
- 8 teaspoons cornstarch mixed with ½ cup water
- 6 teaspoons English mustard

Directions:

1. To make the marinade: Combine brown sugar, oil, lemon juice, pepper, garlic, dried chili flakes, Guinness, water, Worcestershire sauce, salt, soy sauce, and onions in a bowl.

2. Once combined, transfer the marinade into a large Ziploc bag or food-grade plastic bag.

3. Place brisket in the bag and make sure to seal the bag well. Place the bag in the refrigerator for at least 12 hours or longer if possible. Turn the bag over every 30 - 40 minutes.

4. Remove brisket from the marinade and retain the marinade.

5. Set up your smoker and preheat it to 225°F. Place the brisket in a roasting pan in the smoker and smoke the brisket until the internal temperature of the meat in the thickest part shows 160°F to 170°F on an instant-read thermometer or meat thermometer. The approximate timing is 1 - 1 ½ hours of smoking per pound of meat. Add wood chunks or wood chips as and when required. (Follow the manufacturer's instructions on how to use the wood chips). See to it that the temperature of the smoker is maintained between 200°F and 225°F.

6. Once the internal temperature of 160°F is reached, wrap the meat in butcher paper and keep it back in the smoker. When the internal temperature shows 200°F, take it out from the smoker.

7. Do not remove the butcher paper.

8. Wrap the meat with a layer of aluminum foil and keep it in a cooler for resting. Let it rest for 2 - 5 hours.

9. To make the sauce: Pour retained marinade into a saucepan. Add vinegar, cornstarch mixture, and English mustard.

10. Place the saucepan over medium flame. Stir constantly until the sauce is thickened to the desired consistency. Remember, the sauce will thicken even more once cooled.

11. Wrap the meat with a layer of aluminum foil and slice it against the grain and serve with sauce poured on top.

Pulled Chuck Roast with Grilled Onions

Ingredients:

- 2 – 3 chuck roasts (3 pounds each)
- 4 tablespoons Texas style rub or more to taste
- 2 tablespoons olive oil + extra to grill
- Bread slices or burger buns, as required
- ½ teaspoon kosher salt per pound of meat
- 4 medium onions, halved, thinly sliced
- Butter, as needed for the sandwiches
- 1 can cream of mushroom soup
- 2 cans beef broth

Directions:

1. Rub salt all over the chuck roast. Next, rub Texas-style rub all over the roast.

2. Place the roast in a roasting pan and keep it refrigerated for 8 – 9 hours.

3. Start up your smoker and preheat it to 240°F. Place the roasting pan in the smoker and smoke the chuck roast until the internal temperature of the meat in the thickest part shows about 145° – 150°F on an instant-read thermometer or meat thermometer. The approximate timing is 1 – 1 ½ hours of smoking per pound of meat. Add wood chunks or wood chips as and when required. (Follow the manufacturer's instructions on how to use the wood chips). See to it that the temperature of the smoker is maintained between 225°F and 240°F.

4. Pour beef broth and cream of mushroom soup into a large foil pan. Stir until well combined.

5. Now transfer the chuck roast into the foil pan. Keep the foil pan in the smoker and let the meat cook until the internal temperature of the meat shows 175° F in the meat thermometer.

6. Wrap the chuck roast with foil and continue cooking until the internal temperature of the meat shows around 208° F or until the meat is cooked through.

7. Take out the foil pan along with meat from the smoker. Do not unwrap the meat and leave it to rest for 1 – 2 hours.

8. Now unwrap and shred the meat with a pair of forks.

9. Meanwhile, grill the onions in your smoker. For this, drizzle a little oil over the onions and mix well. Place onions on a griddle and grill the onions.

10. Spread butter on both sides of the bread slices and grill the bread slices on the griddle as well.

11. To assemble: Place a little meat and little grilled onions between 2 slices of bread and make sandwiches.

Smoked Lamb Ribs

Ingredients:

- 2 racks lamb ribs, trimmed of fat
- 2 tablespoons onion salt
- 4 teaspoons freshly ground pepper
- 2 tablespoons garlic salt
- 2 tablespoons mixed dried herbs
- Olive oil, as needed

Directions:

1. Combine onion salt, pepper, garlic salt, and mixed dried herbs in a bowl.

2. Take some olive oil and brush it all over the ribs. Cover the ribs with herb mixture. Place it into a roasting pan and let it rest for 30 minutes.

3. Start up your smoker and preheat it to 225°F with indirect cooking. Place the roasting pan in the smoker and roast for 3 – 4 hours.

4. The internal temperature of the meat in the thickest part should show 110°F when the meat is cooked through.

5. Place lamb ribs on your cutting board. When you can manage to handle it, cut the meat between the bones.

6. Serve.

Smoked Meatloaf

Ingredients:

- 4 pounds ground beef
- 4 stalks celery, finely diced
- 6 cloves garlic, minced
- 4 tablespoons Worcestershire sauce
- 2 teaspoons red wine vinegar
- 2 tablespoons minced fresh rosemary
- 3 - 4 teaspoons salt or to taste
- 2 cups onion, finely chopped
- 2 carrots, grated
- 4 cups panko breadcrumbs
- 1 cup red wine
- 6 eggs
- 2 tablespoons minced fresh thyme
- ½ tablespoon paprika
- 1 cup ketchup
- 2 teaspoons olive oil

Directions:

1. Pour oil into a pan and heat over medium-low heat. When the oil is hot, add onion, celery, and carrots and cook until onions are pink.

2. Stir in garlic and sauté for a few seconds until you get a nice aroma. Remove the pan from the heat.

3. Start up your smoker and preheat it to 350°F.

4. Fix the paddle attachment to a mixer. Place ground beef in the mixer and mix. Add sautéed vegetables and mix until well combined. Add an egg and mix well. Repeat this with all the eggs, mixing one at a time and mix well each time.

5. Add thyme, rosemary, wine, breadcrumbs, vinegar, and spices. Mix well.

6. Grease 2 large loaf pans with butter and divide the meat mixture into the pans.

7. Place the loaf pans in the smoker and smoke for 20 minutes. Add wood chunks or wood chips as and when required. (Follow the manufacturer's instructions on how to use the wood chips). See that the temperature of the smoker is maintained between 340°F and 350°F.

8. Remove the loaf pans from the grill and brush ketchup liberally on the top.

9. Smoke for another 10-12 minutes, adding more wood chunks if necessary.

10. Cook until the meat thermometer shows 155 ° F.

Beef Salami

Ingredients:

- 2 pounds ground beef
- 2 teaspoons Morton table salt
- 1 teaspoon freshly ground pepper
- ¼ teaspoon ground nutmeg
- 3 level teaspoons Morton Tender Quick mix
- 1 teaspoon mustard seeds
- 1 teaspoon garlic powder
- ½ teaspoon liquid smoke (optional)

Directions:

1. Combine ground beef, salt, pepper, nutmeg, Morton Tender Quick mix, mustard seeds, garlic powder, and liquid smoke if using in a bowl. Mix until well incorporated.

2. Divide the mixture into four equal portions and shape into logs about 1 ½ inches in diameter.

3. Wrap each portion of the meat in cling wrap or aluminum foil. Keep them in the refrigerator for 8 - 9 hours.

4. Uncover the meat and place them in a broiler pan.

5. Set up the temperature of your oven to 325°F. Place the broiler pan in the oven and bake for 50 - 60 minutes or until the internal temperature of the meat reads 160°F on an instant-read thermometer.

6. Cool completely. Wrap them in foil or cling wrap and keep it refrigerated. You need to consume it within 3 - 5 days. Place it in the freezer if you want it to last longer.

Herbed Sausage

Ingredients:

- 2 pounds lean ground beef
- 4 tablespoons dry red wine
- 2 teaspoons dried basil, crushed
- 1 teaspoon mustard seeds
- ¼ teaspoon onion powder
- 3 level teaspoons Morton Tender Quick mix
- 2 teaspoons freshly ground pepper
- 6 tablespoons grated parmesan cheese
- 2 teaspoons dried oregano, crushed
- ½ teaspoon garlic powder

Directions:

1. Combine ground beef, dry red wine, basil, pepper, onion powder, Morton Tender Quick mix, mustard seeds, parmesan cheese, garlic powder, and oregano in a bowl. Mix until well incorporated.

2. Divide the mixture into four equal portions and shape into logs of about 1 ½ inches diameter.

3. Wrap each portion of the meat in cling wrap or aluminum foil. Keep them in the refrigerator for 8 - 9 hours.

4. Uncover the meat and place them in a broiler pan.

5. Set up the temperature of your oven to 325°F. Place the broiler pan in the oven and bake for 50 - 60 minutes or until the internal temperature of the meat shows 160°F on an instant-read thermometer.

6. Cool completely. Wrap them in foil or cling wrap and keep it refrigerated. You need to consume it within 3 – 5 days. Place it in the freezer if you want it to last longer.

Mexican Chorizo

Ingredients:

- 2.2 pounds pork butt, freshly ground
- 2 teaspoons cayenne pepper
- 2 tablespoons ground cumin
- ½ teaspoon ground cloves
- 2 teaspoons dried oregano
- 2 teaspoons salt
- 6 tablespoons apple cider vinegar
- 2 tablespoons paprika
- 2 tablespoons garlic powder
- 2 teaspoons ground coriander
- 1 teaspoon ground cinnamon
- 1 teaspoon dried thyme
- 1 teaspoon ground black pepper
- Natural hog casing, as required, soaked in water for 30 minutes, drained, rinsed

Directions:

1. Grind the meat in a grinder.
2. Add all the spices and vinegar along with meat and mix on low speed for about 2 minutes.
3. Fill the meat mixture into the hog casings. Twist at the point you would like the length of the sausage to be. Make sure to tie the ends of the sausage.
4. Prick with a sterilized needle wherever you see air pockets. Dry the sausage with a clean towel and hang it in a cool and dry area for 1 hour.

5. Set up your smoker and preheat it to 160°F. Places the sausages in the smoker and smoke them for about 3 – 4 hours or until the internal temperature of the meat in the thickest part shows 160°F on an instant-read thermometer or meat thermometer. Add wood chunks or wood chips as and when required. (Follow the manufacturer's instructions on how to use the wood chips). See that the temperature of the smoker is maintained between 150°F and 160°F.

6. Have an ice bath ready. Remove the sausages from the smoker and immerse them in the ice bath for a while.

Smoked Pastrami

Ingredients:

- 6 – 7 pounds brisket

For pickling spice:

- 1 ½ tablespoons black peppercorns
- 1 ½ tablespoons mustard seeds
- 1 ½ tablespoons allspice berries
- 1 ½ teaspoons ground ginger
- 2 bay leaves, torn
- 1 ½ tablespoons coriander seeds
- 1 ½ tablespoons red chili flakes
- 1 ½ tablespoons whole cloves
- 1 ½ teaspoons ground mace
- 2 sticks cinnamon, crushed

For brine:

- 6 quarts water
- 1 ½ cups white sugar
- 15 cloves garlic, crushed
- 2 ¼ cups kosher salt
- 6 teaspoons pink curing salt (Not Himalayan pink salt)
- 10 pounds ice

For pastrami rub:

- 6 tablespoons black peppercorns
- 2 tablespoons yellow mustard
- 6 tablespoons coriander seeds

Directions:

1. For pickling spice: Combine mustard seeds, coriander seeds, and black peppercorns in a skillet and toast over a high flame until you get a nice aroma, taking care not to burn the spices.

2. Turn off the heat and spread the spice mixture on a napkin. Let it cool for a few minutes.

3. Transfer the spices into a mortar and pound with a pestle until crushed.

4. Transfer the crushed spice into a bowl. Add allspice berries, ginger, bay leaves, chili flakes, cloves, mace, and cinnamon and stir.

5. To make the brine: Pour water into a pot and add white sugar, garlic, kosher salt, pink curing salt, and six tablespoons of the pickling spice mixture.

6. Place the pot over high flame. Stir until sugar and salt dissolve completely. When it begins to boil, turn off the heat.

7. Place ice in a brining bucket. Add brine mixture and let it cool completely—place the brisket in the bucket. Place the bucket in the refrigerator for 4 to 6 days.

8. Take out the brisket from the brine and rinse well under cold running water. Dry the brisket with paper towels.

9. Combine black pepper and coriander in a mortar and pound with a pestle until coarsely ground.

10. Spread a thin layer of yellow mustard all over the brisket. Sprinkle the coriander and pepper mixture all over the brisket.

11. Set up your smoker and preheat it to 250°F. Place the brisket in a roasting pan in the smoker and smoke the brisket for 5 hours.

12. Raise the temperature of the smoker to 300°F. Wrap the brisket with aluminum foil and place it back in the smoker. Smoke for 2 – 3 hours until the internal temperature of the meat in the thickest part shows 160°F on an instant-read thermometer or meat thermometer. (Follow the manufacturer's instructions on how to use the wood chips). See that the temperature of the smoker is maintained between 225°F and 250°F.

13. Unwrap and let it rest for a while

14. Slice the meat against the grain.

Salt Cured Ham (Old-Fashioned Preserving)

Ingredients:
- 6 tablespoons ground red pepper
- 6 cups brown sugar
- 12 cups curing salt
- 6 tablespoons ground black pepper
- 2 fresh hams

Directions:

1. Combine salt, black pepper, red pepper, and brown sugar in a bowl.
2. Rinse the ham with cool water and pat dry with paper towels.
3. Take a deep tray and spread some curing mixture in it. It should be at least ¼ - ½ inch in height from the bottom of the tray.
4. Keep ham over the curing mix in the tray. Make slits at the hipbone and hock joints and pack these slits with curing mix.
5. Sprinkle the remaining curing mix all over the ham and rub it well into it. Place the tray in a cool place for 18 days. Maintain the temperature between 36°F to 40°F. It can be a refrigerator or a cooler with ice in it.
6. Rinse cured ham with cool water and pat dry.
7. The ham is now ready to be smoked.
8. Start up your smoker and preheat it to 225°F. Place the ham in a roasting pan in the smoker and smoke for about 2 hours. Add wood chunks or wood chips as and when required. (Follow the manufacturer's instructions on

how to use the wood chips). See that the temperature of the smoker is maintained between 200°F and 225°F.

9. Now wrap the ham in a double layer of aluminum foil and place it back in the smoker.

10. Smoke the ham until the internal temperature of the meat in the thickest part shows 140°F.

11. Take out the ham from the smoker and let it rest covered in foil for 30 minutes.

12. Slice and serve with the cooked juices collected in the foil.

Canadian Bacon

Ingredients:

- 2 boneless pork loins, trimmed of fat
- 1 teaspoon granulated sugar for every pound of pork loin
- 1 tablespoon Morton Tender Quick mix for every pound of pork loin

Directions:

1. Combine Morton Tender Quick mix and sugar in a bowl. Sprinkle this mixture all over the pork loins and rub it well into the loins.

2. Place the loin in a large Ziploc bag or food-grade plastic bag. Seal the bag tightly and place it in the refrigerator for curing. It should be ready in 3 – 5 days.

3. Take out the meat from the bags and place it in a container filled with cold water.

4. After 30 minutes, remove the loin from the container and dry it with paper towels.

5. Place it on a tray in the refrigerator for some time, so the meat dries a bit.

6. Take out the pork loin and slice it into 1/8-inch-thick slices.

7. Brush a skillet with some oil and heat it over low heat. Cook the meat slices in the pan until brown all over and cook in batches.

8. Serve.

Deli Style Corned Beef

Ingredients:

- 1 beef brisket (8 – 12 pounds), trimmed of fat
- 4 tablespoons brown sugar
- 2 teaspoons ground paprika
- 2 teaspoons ground allspice
- 10 tablespoons Morton Tender Quick mix
- 2 tablespoons ground black pepper
- 2 teaspoons ground bay leaves
- 1 teaspoon garlic powder

Directions:

1. Combine brown sugar, paprika, allspice, Morton Tender Quick mix, pepper, bay leaves, and garlic powder in a bowl.

2. Rub the spice mixture all over the brisket.

3. Place the brisket in a large Ziploc bag or food-grade plastic bag. Seal the bag tightly and place it in the refrigerator for curing. It should take five days for every inch thickness of the meat. So, if the meat is 2 inches thick, it should take ten days.

4. Take out the meat from the bag and place it in a Dutch oven. Pour enough water to cover the meat.

5. Place the Dutch oven over high flame. When the water begins to boil, lower the heat and cook until meat is tender. It should take about 4 to 5 hours.

Pepperoni

Ingredients:

- 2 pounds lean ground beef
- 2 teaspoons liquid smoke
- 1 teaspoon mustard seeds
- ½ teaspoon crushed red pepper
- ½ teaspoon garlic powder
- 3 level teaspoons Morton Tender Quick mix
- 1 ½ teaspoons freshly ground pepper
- 1 teaspoon fennel seeds, lightly crushed
- ½ teaspoon anise seeds

Directions:

1. Combine ground beef, pepper, crushed red pepper, Morton Tender Quick mix, mustard seeds, garlic powder, fennel seeds, anise seeds, and liquid smoke in a bowl. Mix until well incorporated.

2. Divide the mixture into four equal portions and shape into logs of about 1 ½ inches diameter.

3. Wrap each portion of the meat in cling wrap or aluminum foil. Keep them in the refrigerator for 8 – 9 hours.

4. Uncover the meat and place them in a broiler pan.

5. Set up the temperature of your oven to 325°F. Place the broiler pan in the oven and bake for 50 – 60 minutes or until the internal temperature of the meat shows 160°F on an instant-read thermometer.

6. Cool completely. Wrap them in foil or cling wrap and keep it refrigerated. You need to consume it within 3 – 5 days. You can also place it in the freezer, and it will last longer.

German-Style Cured Pork Chops (Gepockelte)

Ingredients:

- 1 tablespoon Morton Tender Quick mix for every pound of chops
- 2 loins or rib chops (about ½ - ¾ inch thick)

Directions:

1. Sprinkle Morton Tender Quick mix all over the chops and rub it well into the loins.
2. Place the loins in a large Ziploc bag or food-grade plastic bag. Seal the bag tightly and place it in the refrigerator for about 2 hours for curing.
3. Take out the meat from the bag and rinse it well with cold running water.
4. Brush a large skillet with some oil and heat it over medium heat. Cook the chops in the pan until brown all over. Pour about half a cup of water and keep the pan covered with a well-fitting lid. Cook until meat is tender, over low heat. It can take about an hour to cook.
5. Serve.

Salt Beef

Ingredients:

For brine:
- 10 cups water
- 4 bay leaves
- 1 teaspoon black peppercorns
- 1 teaspoon ground mace
- 14.1 ounces salt
- 7 ounces sugar
- 6 cloves garlic, sliced

For meat:
- 2.2 pounds beef topside
- 4 stalks celery stalks, coarsely chopped
- 2 onions, chopped
- 4 bay leaves

Directions:

1. To prepare brine: Combine water, bay leaves, black peppercorns, mace, salt, sugar, and garlic in a large saucepan.

2. Place the saucepan over high flame. When the mixture begins to boil, turn off the heat, and let it cool completely.

3. Pour the brine into a stainless-steel container or ceramic container. Place beef in it and keep the container covered in the refrigerator for 8 - 9 hours.

4. Take out the beef from brine and keep it in a large saucepan. Discard the brine. Add onion, bay leaves, and celery, and cover the meat with water. Keep the saucepan over high flame.

5. When the mixture begins to boil, lower the flame, and cook on low heat for a few hours until meat is cooked and tender. It can take 5 – 8 hours.

6. Take out the meat from the saucepan and place it on your cutting board. When cool enough to handle, cut into thin slices.

7. Use it in making sandwiches or serve with mashed potatoes or serve with greens or use in salads.

Cured Corned Beef

Ingredients:

For pickling spices:

- 2 tablespoons whole allspice berries
- 2 tablespoons coriander seeds
- 2 tablespoons whole black peppercorns
- 18 whole cardamom pods
- 4 teaspoons ground ginger
- 2 tablespoons mustard seeds
- 2 tablespoons red pepper flakes
- 4 teaspoons whole cloves
- 12 large bay leaves, crumbled
- 1 stick cinnamon

For brine:

- 1.32 pounds kosher salt or 4 cups Diamond crystal brand kosher salt or 7 tablespoons Morton's kosher salt
- 6 tablespoons pickling spices
- 1 quart water
- 10 teaspoons pink curing salt (not Himalayan pink salt)
- 1 cup brown sugar

For brisket:

- 2 tablespoons pickling spices
- 1 beef brisket (about 9 – 10 pounds)

Directions:

1. To toast spices: Combine allspice berries, coriander seeds, peppercorns, cardamom pods, cloves, red pepper

flakes, and mustard seeds in a pan and toast over medium flame until you get a nice aroma, taking care not to burn the spices. Turn off the heat and transfer it into a mortar.

2. Crush the spices lightly with a pestle and transfer them into a bowl. Add bay leaves and ginger and mix well.

3. To make the brine: Take out about 6 tablespoons of the spice mixture and add into a large pot. Add cinnamon, salt, brown sugar, and water. Place the pot over high flame.

4. When the mixture begins to boil, turn off the heat and let it cool completely. Keep the brine in the refrigerator for 5 – 6 hours.

5. Lay the brisket in a large pan or container. Pour chilled brine over the meat. The meat should be immersed in brine. You can also keep it in a large food-grade plastic bag. Seal the bag tightly and keep the bag in a container.

6. Next, place the brisket in the refrigerator to cure for 5 to 7 days. Turn the brisket over daily. If you have kept it in the plastic bag, turn the bag around once daily.

7. To cook corned beef: Once the brisket is cured, take it out from the brine and rinse it well with cold running water.

8. Place the brisket in a large pot. Pour enough water to cover the meat by at least an inch. If you do not like salty brisket, pour more water into the pot.

9. Stir in pickling spices. Place the pot over high flame. When water boils, cooks on a very low flame until meat is fork-tender.

10. Turn off the heat and cool completely. You can use it now or keep it in the refrigerator for 6 – 7 days.

11. Cut the meat across the grain and serve.

Potato Cakes Stuffed with Cured Meats

Ingredients:

- 2.2 pounds potatoes, peeled, cut into thin slices
- 3 - 4 tablespoons butter
- 7 ounces cheese
- 2 tablespoons olive oil or more if required
- 8 - 12 slices cooked ham or salami or any other cured meat of your choice

Directions:

1. Set up the temperature of the oven to 450°F and preheat it.

2. Add oil and butter into a large ovenproof pan and heat over medium flame. Swirl the pan to mix up oil and melted butter.

3. Place a layer of potatoes all over the bottom of the pan, slightly overlapping, in a clockwise direction. There should be no space between the potato slices.

4. Place another two layers of potatoes similarly over the first layer. Sprinkle salt and pepper over the third layer of potatoes.

5. Next, place half the cured meat over the 3rd layer of potatoes. Place another 2 more layers of potato slices. Sprinkle salt and pepper.

6. Layer with cheese. The next layer will be the remaining meat. Place another 2 - 3 layers of potatoes. Sprinkle salt and pepper. If any more slices of potatoes are remaining, layer them as well. Turn off the heat.

7. Shift the pan into the oven and bake for about 30 minutes or until brown on top and cooked through.

8. Cut into slices and serve.

Stir-Fried Bamboo Shoots and Cured Ham

Ingredients:

- 4 tablespoons vegetable oil
- 6 ounces cured pork belly, thinly sliced
- ½ cup Anhui yellow wine
- 4 green garlic shoots, sliced
- 2 teaspoons cornstarch mixed with ¼ cup water
- 2 inches fresh ginger, peeled, grated
- 4 large fresh bamboo shoots, discard outer leaves, thinly sliced
- ½ teaspoon sugar
- 2 fresh long red chilies, thinly sliced
- Water or stock, as required

Directions:

1. Pour oil into a wok and heat over medium-high flame. When oil is hot, add ginger and stir-fry for about half a minute or until you get a nice aroma.
2. Stir in cured pork belly and cook until brown.
3. Transfer the ginger and pork belly into a bowl and place the wok back over the heat.
4. Place bamboo shoots in the wok. Add a bit of oil if necessary and sauté for a couple of minutes.
5. Stir in sugar, wine, garlic shoots, chili, and stock.
6. Add in cornstarch mixture. Keep stirring until thick. Add cured pork belly mixture and mix well.
7. Serve.

Chapter 12: Fish and Game Recipes

Smoked and Cured Salmon with Orange Zest

Ingredients:
- 2 center-cut salmon fillets (2 pounds each)
- 4 tablespoons light brown sugar
- Zest of 2 oranges, finely grated
- 5 tablespoons kosher salt
- 2 teaspoons ground coriander
- 4 tablespoons vodka

Directions:

1. Spread ½ cup small wood chips on the bottom of the smoker and start it up following the manufacturer's instructions. Set it on high heat.

2. Keep the drip tray and rack over the chips. In a minute or two, smoke will be coming out from the smoker.

3. Lay salmon fillets on the rack, with the skin side down on the rack. Close the smoker and let it smoke for 20 seconds. Shift the salmon away from heat and let it smoke for 30 seconds.

4. Remove salmon fillets from the smoker and keep them in a glass baking dish.

5. Rub the vodka all over the salmon.

6. Then combine brown sugar, salt, orange zest, and coriander in a bowl. Rub this mixture all over the salmon.

7. Cover the dish and place it in the refrigerator. Turn it every day for the next 2 days (3 days in all, from keeping it in the refrigerator to turning it daily for 2 days).

8. Rinse the salmon fillets well with water and pat them dry with paper towels.

9. Cut the salmon into thin slices on the bias and serve.

Smoked Trout

Ingredients:

- 3 trout's (¾ pound each) cleaned
- Salt to taste
- Freshly ground pepper to taste
- 3 lemon halves

Directions:

1. Set up your smoker to 375°F and preheat it. Sprinkle salt and pepper over the trout as well as inside and place it in a pan. Keep the pan in the smoker and smoke the trout for about 30 minutes or until cooked and visibly opaque.

2. Serve with lemon halves.

Smoked Sturgeon

Ingredients:

- 1 ½ - 2 pounds sturgeon, trimmed of fat or dark meat, cut into large rectangular blocks
- 2 tablespoons sugar
- ½ tablespoon garlic powder
- ½ cup kosher salt
- ½ teaspoon ground mace
- 2 - 3 tablespoons whiskey or brandy or more if required

Directions:

1. Combine salt, sugar, garlic powder, and mace in a plastic or stainless-steel container.

2. Place fish pieces in it and turn it around so that the fish is well coated with the curing mixture. If the weight of each block of fish is around 1 pound, cure it for an hour in the refrigerator. If it is ½ pound, cure it for 30 minutes.

3. Place the container in the refrigerator accordingly.

4. Take out the fish blocks from the container and rinse well. Dry the blocks by patting them with paper towels.

5. Place a rack on a baking sheet and place the fish on it. Do not cover the fish. Place the rack along with the baking sheet in the refrigerator for 18 - 24 hours.

6. Start up your smoker and preheat it to 160°F. Place the fish on the rack in the smoker and smoke for 2 - 4 hours, or the way you prefer it to be smoked. Add wood chunks or wood chips as and when required. (Follow the manufacturer's instructions on how to use the wood chips).

See that the temperature of the smoker is maintained between 150°F and 160°F.

7. Once smoked, let it cool completely. Place it in a Ziploc bag or food-grade plastic bag. Remove all the air from the bag. You can vacuum seal the bag if possible and store it until ready to consume.

Smoked King Crab Legs

Ingredients:

- 2 ½ pounds King crab legs

For basting butter:

- ½ cup butter
- 1 tablespoon lemon pepper seasoning
- 2 tablespoons lemon juice
- 1 tablespoon garlic powder or minced garlic

For the spice mix:

- 2 tablespoons salt
- 1 teaspoon paprika
- ½ teaspoon peppercorns
- ½ teaspoon red pepper flakes

Directions:

1. Start up your smoker and preheat it to 225°F.

2. To make basting butter: Combine butter, lemon pepper seasoning, lemon juice, and garlic powder in a microwave-safe bowl. Place the bowl in the microwave. Heat for a few seconds until butter melts.

3. Add salt, paprika, peppercorns, and red pepper flakes into the bowl of the melted butter mixture and stir until well combined.

4. Place crab legs on the rack in the smoker. Smoke for 30 minutes, basting with basting butter mixture every 10 minutes. Add wood chunks or wood chips as and when required. (Follow the manufacturer's instructions on how to use the wood chips). See that the temperature of the smoker is maintained between 200°F and 225°F.

5. Now increase the temperature of the smoker to 350°F. Cook for 2 minutes. Flip sides and cook for another 2 minutes.

6. Serve it right out of the smoker.

Smoked Tilapia

Ingredients:

- 2 tilapia fillets, cleaned, boneless
- Pepper to taste
- 2 cloves garlic, minced
- Lemon slices to serve
- Kosher salt to taste
- 1 tablespoon chopped fresh basil
- ½ tablespoon olive oil

Directions:

1. Start up your smoker and preheat it to 170°F.

2. Mix basil, salt, pepper, olive oil, and garlic in a bowl. Brush this mixture all over the fillets.

3. Place the fish in the smoker and keep the vent open. Add wood chunks or wood chips as and when required. (Follow the manufacturer's instructions on how to use the wood chips). See that the temperature of the smoker is maintained between 160°F and 170°F.

4. Remove it from the smoker after 1-½ hours.

5. Serve with lime slices.

Cured Salmon Gravlax

Ingredients:
- 2 tablespoons white peppercorns, crushed
- 16 ounces rock salt
- 1 salmon (4 pounds), sashimi-grade, skin-on, boneless
- 2 cups chopped dill
- 16 ounces white sugar

For the mustard cream sauce:
- 1 cup heavy cream
- 4 teaspoons mustard powder
- 2/3 cup Dijon mustard or hot mustard
- Salt to taste
- Pepper to taste

To serve:
- Lemon wedges
- Rye bread slices or any other bread slices of your choice, toasted or crackers
- ½ cup chopped dill

Directions:

1. Mix white peppercorns, sugar, salt, and dill in a bowl.

2. Take two large sheets of cling wrap and place them on your countertop in such a manner that they are overlapping slightly.

3. Place half the salt mixture on the cling wrap and spread it so it resembles the salmon.

4. Lay salmon over the salt, with the skin side on the salt. Spread remaining salt all over the salmon.

5. Now cover the salmon with extra cling wrap. If it is not covering completely, use some more cling wrap to wrap up the salmon.

6. Keep the wrapped salmon in a large container. Place a heavy cutting board on the salmon and place 3 - 4 cold drink cans on the cutting board to weigh the salmon down. Keep this entire setup in the refrigerator.

7. After 12 hours, take the salmon and the entire setup out and place it on your countertop.

8. Remove the weights and cutting board. Do not remove the cling wrap.

9. Flip the salmon over and put the cutting board and cold drink cans back over the salmon. Place this entire setup back into the refrigerator.

10. Repeat steps 7 - 9 once again, so in all, this curing process is to be done for 36 hours. This is a medium cure.

11. Remove the cling wrap and remove the excess salt mixture by scraping it off. Rinse the salmon well and dry it by patting it with paper towels.

12. If you have time, place the salmon in a container and place it in the refrigerator for 3 to 12 hours. Do not cover the salmon this time and let it dry.

13. Cut the salmon at an angle. You are not supposed to eat the skin, so cut it accordingly.

14. To make the mustard sauce: Combine heavy cream, mustard powder, Dijon mustard, salt, and pepper in a bowl.

15. Serve salmon slices with bread. Scatter dill on top. Serve with mustard sauce and lemon wedges.

Kelp-Cured Blue Mackerel with Fennel Salad

Ingredients:

- 1 whole blue mackerel, headless, remove pin bones, gutted, made into 2 fillets
- ½ cup rice wine vinegar
- ½ teaspoon brine from a jar of preserved lemons
- ½ tablespoons finely chopped chives
- 3 tablespoons broken pomelo segments
- ½ tablespoon fine salt
- 2 sheets dried kelp (kombu)
- Extra-virgin olive oil, to drizzle
- Microgreens like red garnets, shallots, etc.

For dressing:

- 1 tablespoon mirin
- ¼ teaspoon finely chopped red Asian shallots
- 2 tablespoons soy sauce
- ¼ teaspoon finely grated ginger
- ½ teaspoon finely grated lemon zest

For salad:

- 1 young fennel bulb, shaved
- 1 tablespoon fresh lemon juice
- Salt to taste
- Freshly ground black pepper to taste
- ¾ tablespoon extra-virgin olive oil

Directions:

1. With the flesh side facing up, lay the fish fillets on a tray. Sprinkle it with salt. Keep in the refrigerator for 30 minutes.

2. Add rice wine vinegar into a bowl. Dip the fish fillets in the vinegar one at a time and keep them on a plate—brush remaining vinegar over the kelp sheets.

3. Brush lemon juice on the flesh side of mackerel and keep each on a piece of kelp, with the flesh side touching the kelp.

4. Cover mackerel with the remaining 2 pieces of kelp and place them on a tray. Keep the tray covered with cling wrap and keep it in the refrigerator for 3 – 8 hours, depending on how much time you have on hand.

5. To make the dressing: Whisk together mirin, shallots, soy sauce, ginger, and lemon zest in a bowl. Cover and set aside for a couple of hours for the flavors to fuse.

6. Sprinkle salt and pepper over the fennel. Drizzle lemon juice and olive oil over the fennel and toss well. Spread over a serving platter.

7. Discard the skin from the mackerel and cut it into very thin slices across the grain.

8. Place mackerel slices over the fennel—drizzle dressing over the fennel and mackerel.

9. Sprinkle chives, pommel, and microgreens over the salad. Trickle some extra-virgin olive oil on top and serve.

Marinated and Smoked Venison Tenderloin

Ingredients:

- 4 venison tenderloins (6 - 8 ounces each) remove silver skins
- ½ cup extra-virgin olive oil
- 2 teaspoon brown or Dijon mustard
- 1 small onion, diced
- 2 teaspoons dried rosemary
- 2 teaspoons cracked black pepper
- 2/3 cup dry red wine
- 2 tablespoons soy sauce or tamari
- 2 teaspoons honey or maple syrup
- 4 cloves garlic, minced
- 2 teaspoons sea salt

Directions:

1. Combine olive oil, mustard, onion, rosemary, pepper, red wine, soy sauce, honey, garlic, and sea salt in a bowl.
2. Take 2 - 3 large Ziploc bags and put the tenderloins in them. Drizzle the marinade over the tenderloins. Seal the bags after removing extra air from the bags.
3. With the bag sealed, massage the meat so that the meat is coated with the marinade. Keep the bags in a dish and chill for 8 - 12 hours.
4. About 20 minutes before starting the smoker, take out the meat from the refrigerator.
5. Take out a grill rack from the smoker and place it over paper towels.

6. Set up your smoker and preheat it to 250°F. Keep the top vent open. Place the venison on the rack and discard the marinade. Place the rack in the smoker and smoke the venison until the internal temperature of the meat in the thickest part shows between 140°F - 150°F on an instant-read thermometer or meat thermometer, depending on how you like it cooked. Add wood chunks or wood chips as and when required. (Follow the manufacturer's instructions on how to use the wood chips). See that the temperature of the smoker is maintained between 240°F and 225°F. It should be cooked in 2 - 2 ½ hours.

7. Once cooked, place the venison on your cutting board. Cover loosely with foil.

8. After about 20 - 25 minutes, cut into thin slices and serve with a side dish of your choice.

Smoked Venison Jerky

Ingredients:

- 10 pounds venison meat, trimmed of fat, rinsed, cut into ¼ inch thick slices across the grain
- 1 cup water
- 1 cup soy sauce
- ½ cup brown sugar
- 2 tablespoons Morton Tender Quick mix
- 3 teaspoons Cajun spice mix
- 2 tablespoons garlic powder
- 2 teaspoons cayenne pepper
- 2 tablespoons ground black pepper
- 2 teaspoons celery salt

Directions:

1. Combine water, soy sauce, Morton Tender Quick mix, brown sugar, Cajun spice mix, garlic powder, cayenne pepper, black pepper, and celery salt in a bowl. Stir until brown sugar, and Morton Tender Quick mix dissolves completely.

2. Place venison in a large bowl. Drizzle half the marinade over it and stir until well combined.

3. Drizzle the remaining marinade over the venison and stir until well combined. Set aside for a couple of hours to soak.

4. Grease the smoker racks with some oil. Place the racks over baking sheets. Place the venison strips along with the marinade in a colander to drain.

5. Set up your smoker and preheat it to 200°F. Place meat strips on the racks and keep the racks in the smoker, along with the baking sheets. Smoke for 3 - 4 hours or until dry and a bit pliant as well. Add wood chunks or wood chips as and when required. (Follow the manufacturer's instructions on how to use the wood chips). See that the temperature of the smoker is maintained between 160°F and 200°F. It can take anywhere between 2 - 6 hours or longer.

6. Take out the jerky from the smoker and cool completely. Transfer into an airtight container or Ziploc bag. You can use it after one day because the meat will soak in the smoke.

Brined and Smoked Wild Boar Shoulder Roast

Ingredients:
- 8 – 12 pounds wild boar shoulder roast
- 2 cups brown sugar
- 1 cup soy sauce or tamari
- 4 tablespoons cracked pepper
- 4 bay leaves
- 2 gallons filtered water
- 1 ½ cups kosher salt
- ½ cup Worcestershire sauce
- 2 tablespoons dried rosemary
- Apple cider for smoking

Directions:

1. Pour water into a large stockpot and bring to a boil over a high flame. Remove the pot from heat. Add salt and sugar into the pot and stir until the sugar dissolves completely.

2. Let the mixture cool completely.

3. Stir in soy sauce, pepper, bay leaves, Worcestershire sauce, and rosemary. Add the meat into the pot. Now transfer the meat along with brine into a large, food-grade plastic bag that can be sealed. You can also keep it in a container but make sure that it isn't aluminum.

4. After sealing the bag, place it in a cooler or refrigerator for 6 – 8 hours.

5. About 25 minutes before starting the smoker, take out the meat from the refrigerator.

6. Take out the grill rack from the smoker. After rinsing the meat under cold running water, pat it dry with paper towels. Discard the brine.

7. Place the meat on the rack.

8. Add apple cider to the bowl of water in the smoker.

9. Start up your smoker and preheat it to 275°F. Keep the top vent open. Place the boar on the rack. Place rack in the smoker and smoke the boar until the internal temperature of the meat in the thickest part shows between 145°F - 155°F for sliced meat, or 160°F - 165°F for pulled boar on an instant-read thermometer or meat thermometer, depending on how you like it cooked. Add wood chunks or wood chips, water, and apple cider as and when required. (Follow the manufacturer's instructions on how to use the wood chips). See that the temperature of the smoker is maintained between 260°F and 275°F. It should be cooked in 4 - 5 hours.

10. Once cooked, place the boar on your cutting board. Cover loosely with foil.

11. After 20 - 25 minutes, cut into thin slices or shred with a pair of forks and serve with a side dish of your choice. You can also serve it with **BBQ** sauce.

Smoked Whole Quail

Ingredients:

- 3 whole quails, skin-on, cleaned
- 1 teaspoon sea salt
- ½ teaspoon garlic powder
- ¼ teaspoon dried oregano
- ¼ teaspoon dried thyme
- ½ apple, cored, cut into 3 equal slices
- 4 teaspoons extra-virgin olive oil
- ½ teaspoon cracked black pepper
- ½ teaspoon smoked paprika
- Zest of 1/8 lemon, grated

Directions:

1. Place thyme, oregano, pepper, paprika, lemon zest, garlic powder, and sea salt in a container.

2. Place quails in the container and turn them around in the brining mixture. Rub the brining mixture into the quails.

3. Cover and chill for 4 – 6 hours in the refrigerator.

4. About 25 minutes before starting the smoker, take out the quails from the refrigerator.

5. Take out the grill rack from the smoker. After rinsing the quails under cold running water, pat them dry with paper towels. Discard the brine.

6. Place the quails on the rack.

7. Add apple cider to the bowl of water in the smoker.

8. Set up your smoker and preheat it to 220°F. Keep the top vent open. Fill a slice of apple in the cavity of each quail. Keep the quails on the rack. Place a rack in the smoker and smoke the quails until the internal temperature of the meat in the thickest part shows between 145°F - 155°F on an instant-read thermometer or meat thermometer, depending on how you like it cooked. Add wood chunks or wood chips as and when required. (Follow the manufacturer's instructions on how to use the wood chips). See that the temperature of the smoker is maintained between 200°F and 220°F. It should be cooked in 4 - 5 hours.

9. Once cooked, place the quails on your cutting board. Cover loosely with foil.

10. It is best served with wild rice or brown rice, or a mixture of both. You can also serve it with a salad made of wild rice.

Smoked Pheasant Breast

Ingredients:

- 2 pheasant breasts
- ½ cup chopped fresh basil
- ½ tablespoon salt
- 2 rashers middle bacon
- Ground black pepper to taste
- 1 cup water

Directions:

1. Combine water and salt in a bowl. Stir until salt dissolves completely. Place the pheasant breasts in the bowl in the refrigerator for 4 to 6 hours.

2. Set up your smoker and preheat it to 225°F.

3. Place the pheasant breasts on the cooking plank. Sprinkle pepper over the breasts and scatter basil on top. Place bacon slices to cover the breasts and tuck the ends beneath the breasts.

4. Smoke for 2 hours. Add wood chunks or wood chips as and when required. (Follow the manufacturer's instructions on how to use the wood chips). See that the temperature of the smoker is maintained between 210°F and 225°F. Once cooked, take it out of the smoker and place it on your cutting board.

5. When cool enough to handle, cut into pieces and serve.

Smoked Duck Breast

Ingredients:

- 1 duck breast half (about ¾ pound)
- 2 cups apple juice or apple cider
- ½ bay leaf, crushed
- ¼ teaspoon whole peppercorns, cracked
- 2 tablespoons kosher salt or 1 ½ tablespoons canning salt
- 2 small cloves garlic, crushed
- Melted bacon grease, as required

Directions:

1. Combine apple juice, bay leaf, peppercorns, kosher salt, and garlic in a bowl.

2. Drop the duck breast half in the brine and let it soak for 2 - 8 hours, depending on how much time you have.

3. Take out the breast half from the brine and rinse under cold running water. Now pat dry with paper towels.

4. Smear melted bacon grease all over the breast half.

5. Set up your smoker and preheat it to 225°F. Place the duck breast half in the smoker and smoke for 1 - 2 hours. Add wood chunks or wood chips as and when required. (Follow the manufacturer's instructions on how to use the wood chips). See that the temperature of the smoker is maintained between 200°F and 225°F.

6. Cook until the internal temperature of the meat in the thickest part shows between 155°F - 165°F on an instant-read thermometer or meat thermometer, depending on how you like it cooked.

7. It is best served with wild rice or brown rice, or a mixture of both.

Maple-Smoked Duck Breasts

Ingredients:

- 4 boneless duck breast halves, skin-on
- 4 teaspoons cracked black pepper
- 2 teaspoons maple syrup to brush
- 6 tablespoons maple syrup
- 4 tablespoons kosher salt

Directions:

1. Sprinkle salt and pepper all over the duck breast halves. Place them in a dish and drizzle 6 tablespoons of maple syrup over them.

2. Cover the dish and chill for 12 – 24 hours.

3. Set up your smoker and preheat it to 225°F. Place the duck breast halves in the smoker and smoke for 3 – 4 hours. Add maple wood chunks or wood chips as and when required. (Follow the manufacturer's instructions on how to use the wood chips). See that the temperature of the smoker is maintained between 200°F and 225°F.

4. Cook until the internal temperature of the meat in the thickest part shows between 155°F - 165°F on an instant-read thermometer or meat thermometer, depending on how you like it cooked.

5. Cool completely. Cut into slices. It is now ready to serve.

6. Store the leftovers in an airtight container in the refrigerator. It can last for 4 – 5 days.

Goose Pastrami

Ingredients:

- 4 skinless goose breasts
- ½ teaspoon pink curing salt (not Himalayan pink salt) for every 3 pounds of goose breasts
- ½ teaspoon celery seeds
- 2 teaspoons sugar
- 2 tablespoons +2 teaspoons ground black pepper
- 2 tablespoons ground coriander
- 1 teaspoon dried thyme
- ½ teaspoon caraway seeds
- ½ teaspoon crushed juniper berries (optional)
- ½ cup brandy or red wine or water or vinegar
- 1 tablespoon kosher salt for every pound of goose meat

Directions:

1. You can use slightly lesser salt if desired. Once you weigh the goose breasts, use kosher salt and curing salt accordingly.

2. Combine curing salt, kosher salt, thyme, sugar, caraway, celery seeds, 2 teaspoons black pepper, and juniper berries in a spice grinder and grind until you get a powder consistency.

3. Cover the goose breasts with the spice mixture. Rub the mixture into the meat. Place them in an airtight container and keep them in the refrigerator for 24 – 72 hours.

4. Take goose breasts out of the refrigerator and rinse well with cold running water. Pat dry with paper towels.

5. Place a rack on a baking sheet and put the goose breast halves on it. Place it in the refrigerator and let it dry in the refrigerator for 24 hours.

6. Pour brandy or red wine or vinegar or water into a container. Place the goose breast halves in the container for a few seconds.

7. Take it out and sprinkle 2 tablespoons of pepper over the breasts. Also, sprinkle ground coriander.

8. Set up your smoker and preheat it to 225°F. Place the duck breast halves in the smoker and smoke for 3 – 4 hours. Add maple wood chunks or wood chips as and when required. (Follow the manufacturer's instructions on how to use the wood chips). See to it that the temperature of the smoker is maintained between 200°F and 225°F.

9. Cook until the internal temperature of the meat in the thickest part shows between 140°F on an instant-read thermometer or meat thermometer, depending on how you like it cooked.

10. Cool completely. Slice the meat against the grain.

11. Store leftovers in an airtight container in the refrigerator. It can last for 5 – 6 days.

Smoked Cornish Game Hens

Ingredients:

- 1 Cornish game hen
- ½ tablespoon salt
- ½ tablespoon dried basil
- ½ teaspoon dried thyme
- ½ teaspoon dried oregano
- ½ teaspoon cayenne pepper
- 1 tablespoon butter, melted
- 1 teaspoon ground black pepper

Directions:

1. Dry the Cornish game hen by patting with paper towels.

2. Smear butter all over the hen and rub it well into it.

3. Set up your smoker and preheat it to 275°F. Place the Cornish game hen in the smoker and smoke for 1 - 2 hours. Add wood chunks or wood chips as and when required. (Follow the manufacturer's instructions on how to use the wood chips). See to it that the temperature of the smoker is maintained between 260°F and 275°F.

4. Cook until the internal temperature of the meat in the thickest part shows 180°F on an instant-read thermometer or meat thermometer.

Wild Game Backstrap

Ingredients:

- 2 pounds elk or deer backstrap or tenderloin
- ¾ cup butter
- 3 sprigs rosemary
- 4 cloves garlic, sliced
- Coarse salt to taste
- Ground black pepper to taste
- 2 tablespoons olive oil or as much as needed

Directions:

1. Brush olive oil lightly all over the backstrap. Sprinkle salt and pepper over it.

2. Set up your smoker and preheat it to 225°F. Place the meat in the smoker and smoke for 1 – 2 hours. Add wood chunks or wood chips as and when required. (Follow the manufacturer's instructions on how to use the wood chips). See that the temperature of the smoker is maintained between 200°F and 225°F.

3. Cook until the internal temperature of the meat in the thickest part shows 100°F on an instant-read thermometer or meat thermometer.

4. Remove the meat from the smoker.

5. Meanwhile, make garlic herb butter: Combine ½ cup butter, half the garlic, and 2 sprigs of rosemary in a small pot.

6. Place the pot over low flame, let the butter melt, and cook for 3 to 4 minutes.

7. Turn off the heat and set it aside.

8. Place a cast-iron skillet over medium flame. Add ¼ cup butter, remaining garlic, and rosemary, and let the butter melt.

9. Place backstrap in the pan and cook the meat until you have a crust on the meat. Use the butter from the same pan to baste while cooking. Cook until the internal temperature of the meat in the thickest part shows 125°F on an instant-read thermometer or meat thermometer.

10. Take out the meat from the pan and place it on your cutting board. When it cools a bit, cut into about ¼ inch thick slices.

11. Spread the garlic herb butter over the meat. Sprinkle salt on top and serve.

Sugar Cured Feral Hog

Ingredients:
- 4 – 6 pounds ham
- 1 cup sugar
- 1 cup sea salt or kosher salt
- 12 – 16 cups cold water

For basting:
- ½ jar Texas Gourmet's Mandarin orange Serrano jelly
- 1 ½ teaspoons finely chopped rosemary leaves
- ¼ cup olive oil
- 1 ½ tablespoons soy sauce
- ½ tablespoon ground ginger
- 3 ounces Crown Royal whiskey
- 2 tablespoons honey
- ¼ cup butter
- 1 tablespoon ground black pepper
- 3 cloves garlic, peeled, minced

Directions:

1. For curing: Combine sugar, salt, and cold water in a container and stir until sugar and salt dissolve completely.

2. Place the ham in a Ziploc bag or food-grade plastic bag. Take your turkey injector and inject 2 – 3 full injectors of the solution into the ham at different places and adjacent to the bone.

3. Pour the remaining solution into the bag. Remove air from the bag and seal it up tightly.

4. Keep the bag in the refrigerator for 24 - 48 hours, depending on how much time you have.

5. Take out the ham from the solution and rinse it well under cold running water. Pat dry with paper towels.

6. To make basting mixture: Combine jelly, rosemary leaves, oil, soy sauce, ginger, whiskey, butter, pepper, and garlic in a bowl.

7. Start up your smoker and preheat it to 275°F. Place the ham in the smoker and smoke the ham roast until the internal temperature of the meat in the thickest part shows about 160°F on an instant-read thermometer or meat thermometer. The approximate timing is about 45 minutes of smoking per pound of meat. Add wood chunks or wood chips as and when required. (Follow the manufacturer's instructions on how to use the wood chips). See to it that the temperature of the smoker is maintained between 250°F and 275°F.

8. As the ham is smoked, you must baste it as well. Baste with the basting mixture every 45 minutes. Turn the ham after every 1-½ hour.

9. Once cooked, remove ham from the smoker and place it on your cutting board. Cover it loosely with foil. Let it rest for 45 minutes.

10. Slice and serve with the remaining basting mixture.

Smoked Mackerel Salad

Ingredients:

- 2 smoked mackerel fillets, flaked
- 3 – 4 cups baby spinach
- 4 cherry tomatoes, halved
- ½ large bag salad leaves, torn
- 4 boiled new potatoes, sliced

For dressing:

- ½ tablespoon balsamic vinegar
- ½ teaspoon honey
- 2 tablespoons extra-virgin olive oil
- ½ teaspoon Dijon mustard

Directions:

1. To make the dressing: Whisk together vinegar, honey, oil, and Dijon mustard in a bowl.

2. Place salad leaves, spinach, and potatoes in a bowl and toss well.

3. Pour half the dressing over the salad and toss well.

4. Distribute the salad between 2 plates, top with the mackerel and tomatoes and drizzle the remaining dressing on top. Serve immediately.

Conclusion

Preserving food using different techniques is not a modern concept. Our early ancestors were known to freeze meats on ice in extremely cold climatic conditions and sun-drying foods in tropical and hot regions. Initially, food preservation was more about survival than taste or flavor. Food preservation techniques also reduce the risk of food spoilage or contamination. What more? Smoked and cured meats, fish, and poultry have proved to be incredibly delicious.

Smoking and curing are not difficult techniques. Once you get the hang of it, you will realize how simple it truly is. From understanding the basic elements of these techniques to their nuances, everything you need to know is given within this book. You can start making delicious mouthwatering meals quickly at home using the recipes in this book!

Now that you have all the information you need, what are you waiting for? Gather the required supplies and ingredients, select a recipe that strikes your fancy, and follow the simple instructions in this book. To master the art of smoking and curing, you need a little patience and the right information. Now that you have everything needed, it is time to learn and experiment!

Thank you, and all the best!

Here's another book by Dion Rosser that you might like

GROWING POTATOES

HOW TO GROW POTATOES IN CONTAINERS, RAISED BEDS, BAGS, THE GROUND AND MORE ALONG WITH TIPS FOR HARVESTING AND STORING

DION ROSSER

References

Carole, C. (n.d.). An overview of 10 home food preservation methods from ancient to modern. Retrieved from Homepreservingbible.com website: http://www.homepreservingbible.com/630-an-overview-of-10-home-food-preservation-methods-from-ancient-to-modern/

Christine Venema, Michigan State University Extension. (n.d.). Smoking as a food cooking method - MSU Extension. Retrieved from Msu.edu website: https://www.canr.msu.edu/news/smoking_as_a_food_cooking_method

Coppieters, K. (2014, April 23). The science of curing meats safely. Retrieved from Amazingribs.com website: https://amazingribs.com/tested-recipes/salting-brining-curing-and-injecting/curing-meats-safely

Curing and smoking meats for home food preservation. (n.d.). Retrieved from Uga.edu website: https://nchfp.uga.edu/publications/nchfp/lit_rev/cure_smoke_pres.html

Curing and smoking poultry. (2019, February 11). Retrieved from Tamu.edu website: https://agrilifeextension.tamu.edu/library/health-nutrition/curing-and-smoking-poultry/

Food preservation: History, methods, types. (2011, August 22). Retrieved from Schoolworkhelper.net website: https://schoolworkhelper.net/food-preservation-history-methods-types/

How to smoke fish – step-by-step guide. (2017, November 10). Retrieved from Cavetools.com website: https://blog.cavetools.com/how-to-smoke-fish/

Introduction and definition of food preservation. (n.d.). Retrieved from Brainkart.com website: https://www.brainkart.com/article/Introduction-and-Definition-of-Food-Preservation_33475/

Laurie Messing, Michigan State University Extension. (n.d.). The history of preserving food at home - Safe Food & Water. Retrieved from Msu.edu website: https://www.canr.msu.edu/news/food_preservation_is_as_old_as_mankind

MGConsults. (2017a, October 10). Advantages & disadvantages of food smoking - SmokeHouseReview. Retrieved from Smokehousereview.com website: http://smokehousereview.com/2017/10/10/advantages-disadvantages-of-food-smoking/

MGConsults. (2017b, October 10). Basic food smoking tips. - SmokeHouseReview. Retrieved from Smokehousereview.com website: http://smokehousereview.com/2017/10/10/basic-food-smoking-tips/

MGConsults. (2017c, October 13). Types of wood used for food smoking. - SmokeHouseReview. Retrieved from Smokehousereview.com website: http://smokehousereview.com/2017/10/13/types-of-wood-used-for-food-smoking/

PaulTM, & ARNIE. (2016, May 22). How is smoking used for food processing and preservation? Retrieved from Foodsafetyhelpline.com website: https://foodsafetyhelpline.com/smoking-used-food-processing-preservation/

Proper processing of wild game and fish. (n.d.). Retrieved from Psu.edu website: https://extension.psu.edu/proper-processing-of-wild-game-and-fish

Restaurant Business Staff. (2010, May 1). The art and science of smoking foods. Retrieved from Restaurantbusinessonline.com website: https://www.restaurantbusinessonline.com/art-science-smoking-foods

Riches, D. (n.d.). Smoked fish: A centuries-old tradition. Retrieved from Thespruceeats.com website: https://www.thespruceeats.com/guide-to-smoking-fish-331552

Vuković, D. (2019, June 17). The 3 methods of curing meat with salt. Retrieved from Primalsurvivor.net website: https://www.primalsurvivor.net/salt-curing/

Waggoner, C. (2016, June 2). 5 ways to tell if food has gone bad, because no one trusts expiration dates. Retrieved from Spoonuniversity.com website: https://spoonuniversity.com/how-to/food-gone-bad-ways-to-tell

(N.d.-a). Retrieved from Suburbansteader.com website: https://www.suburbansteader.com/introduction-food-preservation/

(N.d.-b). Retrieved from Asgmag.com website: https://www.asgmag.com/prepping/smoke-em-6-steps-to-preserve-meat-through-smoking/

(N.d.-c). Retrieved from Masterclass.com website: https://www.masterclass.com/articles/what-is-a-bbq-smoker-6-types-of-meat-smokers-and-the-best-smoker-for-texas-style-barbecue#types-of-smokers-direct-vs-indirect-heat

Printed in Great Britain
by Amazon